The *Deeper* Secret Teachings
------------of------------
CHRIST

MARK K. OLSEN

Copyright © 2025 by Mark K. Olsen.

ISBN: 979-8-89090-818-6 (sc)
ISBN: 979-8-89090-445-4 (hb)
ISBN: 979-8-89090-819-3 (e)

All rights reserved. No part of this book may be reproduced or transmitted in any form or by any means, electronic or mechanical, including photocopying, recording, or by any information storage and retrieval system, without permission in writing from the copyright owner.

EXPRESSO
Executive Center 777, Dunsmuir Street Vancouver, BC V71K4
1-888-721-0662 ext 101
info@expressopublishing.com

Dedicated to Gary D Olsen, a warrior for God.

CONTENTS

INTRODUCTION v
THE SECRET TEACHINGS 1
ONE'S TRUE IDENTITY 5
THE PROCESS OF SOUL'S GROWTH 11
THE SEVEN HEAVENS OF CREATION. 15
    The First Heaven. 32
    The Second Heaven 39
    The Third Heaven 44
    The Fourth Heaven. 49
    The Fifth Heaven 56
    The Sixth Heaven 61
    The Seventh Heaven 64
    The Heart Of God 68
BECOMING CLOSE TO CHRIST 71
    Accepting Christ. 71
    Commitment: 74
    Study. 78
    Devotions 83
    Prayer 89
    Listening. 91
    Love 93
    Creative imagination. 95
    Self-surrender 96
    Freedom 100
    The shadow, or dark side. .101
    Worship of the personality 103
    The feminine believer 105

    Detachment 105
    Dreams and visions. 107
    Faith 110
    Present Times 114

Conclusion 117

GLOSSARY 119

THE SEVEN HEAVENS OF CREATION. 125

INTRODUCTION

The deeper secret teachings have been existent forever, as Christ has existed forever: the Christ in Jesus merely restated them anew. These teachings, often called esoteric or hidden, exist in every known religion, and in Christianity, are often associated with Gnosticism, which began as a competing school of Christian thought when the disciples of Christ still walked the Earth. However, the deeper secrets begin where Gnosticism leaves off.

These teachings emphasize going inside oneself to find Christ, and one's self, through direct personal experience and revelation. While the secret doctrine differs somewhat from mainstream Christian beliefs, the practices are virtually the same: accepting Christ as one's personal savior and guide, daily devotions, prayer, contemplation of scripture, study, and listening to the Word. There are not leaders or churches in the secret teachings, as direct personal revelation is emphasized; it is a solitary adventure.

For thousands of years these teachings were passed down orally, as persecution was, and is, a constant danger. However, in the Western world today, this is less of a problem, as freedom of speech, (within limits) and freedom of religion, have been enshrined as basic human rights. One of the many effects from these freedoms, is an enormous explosion of esoteric paths and literature; this has brought many of these protected beliefs out into the open for anyone to access. This has primarily included the lighter secret teachings of Christ, which are now available from groups and books all over the globe.

Many of the more profound secrets within these beliefs still require the spiritual experiences that reveal them, and often times, specific doctrines and realizations remain "secret," through a lack of individual understanding and direct personal experience.

"But the natural man receiveth not the things of the Spirit of God: for they are foolishness unto him: neither can he know *them,* because they are spiritually discerned." (I Corinthians 2:14)

In this brief overview of the deeper secret teachings, they will be examined in five areas:

1) The secret teachings in Christianity.
2) One's true identity.
3) The process of soul's growth.
4) The seven levels of heaven.
5) Becoming closer to Christ.

Support and evidence of these deeper teachings, will rely on over four hundred verses from the King James' translation of the Christian Holy Bible, and several verses from the Gospel of St. Thomas, which is generally thought to be the earliest and most authentic of the gospels. The secret teachings do not favor modern translations; while they are well-intentioned, and do make some passages easier to understand, there are serious omissions of words and phrases that have double meanings, or hidden significance.

The purpose of this book is to inform, encourage, and inspire those who are looking for a deep relationship with the living Christ. The ideas presented are not the author's, although he does subscribe to them; these truths are universal and eternal, and are secretly taught all over the globe.

THE SECRET TEACHINGS

The first question which may come up concerning secret teachings, is whether any such teachings exist in Christianity. This can be answered from a number of directions by consulting the Holy Christian Bible.

One indication that there are indeed deeper teachings, comes from the fact that Christ in Jesus spoke to the masses only in parable, refusing to discuss secrets the public could not understand.

Christ Jesus explains this to His disciples: "And he said, Unto you it is given to know the mysteries of the kingdom of God: but to others in parables; that seeing they might not see, and hearing they might not understand." (Luke 8:10)

In addition, Christ Jesus refers to the people as "a generation of vipers" (Mark 12:34) who can perceive nothing, and while explaining His parables to the disciples, (Mark 4:34) refuses to talk plainly to the public.

"All these things spake Jesus unto the multitude in parables; and without a parable spake he not unto them…." (Matthew 13:34)

St. Paul also speaks of the mysteries that have remained secret "since the foundation of the world…," (Romans 16:25) and only … "now have been made manifest to his saints." (Colossians 1:27)

The Christ in Jesus states: "I shall give you what no eye has seen and what no ear has heard, and what no hand has touched…and what has never occurred to the human mind." (Gospel of St. Thomas #7)

A reason that deeper teachings remained secret, and only given orally to a select few, was due to a fear of persecution, and even though the Christ in Jesus and His disciples were circumspect in what deeper teachings they revealed, they were all, along with tens of thousands of early Christians, tortured and killed in the most horrible of ways. In addition, any writings that differed from what early leaders considered orthodox, were considered blasphemous and burned.

This begs the question: If deep secrets do indeed exist in Christianity, what are they? and how do they differ from today's mainstream interpretation of Christ Jesus' message?

Perhaps as a beginning, it might be helpful to present the esoteric definition of Christ, as this is perhaps a main difference between esoteric (hidden) and exoteric (mainstream) Christianity.

The secret teachings believe that Christ is a Spirit, the Son of God, the Christ consciousness, and is not a person, but that Christ is everything created by Christ, as He created everything out of Himself as the Holy Word. This wondrous power gradually steps down in vibration as it emanates from the center, fashioning the seven planes of heaven and everything in them, including humanity.

St. John writes: "All things were made by him; and without him was not anything made that was made." (John 1:3)

In addition, St. Paul states that the secret and mystery of the ages has been revealed, that "Christ [is] in you…." (Colossians 1:27) This means that Christ is in everyone, everywhere; if entities exist on other worlds, as the secret teachings believe, Christ is in them too; He also created them.

St. Paul confirms this in Colossians 3:11, when he states that …" Christ *is* all, and *in* all." This should settle any doubts, and means that there is nothing that is not Christ, including all of the souls, planets, stars, and galaxies, not only in the first heaven, but in all of the seven heavens; in short, anything that has existence. This also means that Christ is *thee* Son of God, and the entirety of the Holy Word, which emanates from the ALMIGHTY ABSOLUTE GOD.

Several decades ago, scientists at a prestigious university in Los Angeles, California, extracted one cell from a donor carrot, and proceeded to grow an entire carrot from that one cell: in other words, the one cell of the donor carrot was a microcosm of the entire carrot, the macrocosm. Such a relationship also exists between soul, the microcosm, and the body of Christ, the macrocosm.

Soul is one cell of the body of Christ, and over eternity can grow Christ-like, reflecting the attributes and characteristics of the overall existent Christ. Souls have the divine potential to reach the Christ consciousness in the seventh heaven, and become one with Christ.

As St. Paul states: "So we, being many, are one body in Christ, and everyone members, one of another." (Romans 12:5)

Luke writes: "For in him we live, and move, and have our being." (Acts 17:28)

The secret teachings believe that Christ is a raging inferno of love, wisdom, power and freedom, infinite in all directions, and that the individual soul is one spark of that holy fire, one drop of that infinite ocean, one cell of that wondrous consciousness and power called Christ. Nothing more, *but* nothing less.

Christ is infinitely greater than can be imagined, and as the Son of God is beyond one's comprehension. The secret teachings believe that soul, over eternities, climbs Jacob's ladder, gradually traversing the planes of heaven one by one; eventually, soul arrives at the top of the seventh heaven, and becomes fully one with Christ, a son of God.

"But as many as received him, to them gave he power to become sons of God, *even* to them that believe on his name." (John 1:12)

One of the primary pillars of esoteric belief is that to find Christ, salvation, and oneself, it is mandatory to go inside oneself. To be clear, going inside simply means looking inside, often times with one's eyes closed, like many people do in prayer. It can also include daydreaming, spacing out, reflecting, pondering, meditating, imagining, musing, or looking into one's mind's eye.

The Christ in Jesus makes this stunningly clear: "And when he was demanded of the Pharisees, when the kingdom of God should come, he answered them and said, the kingdom of God cometh not with observation: Neither shall they say, Lo here! Or lo there! For, behold, the kingdom of God is within you." (Luke 17:20-21)

If the kingdom of God is within one, as the Christ in Jesus states, and Christ is in one, as St. Paul states, (Colossians 1:27) who might one expect to meet when looking inside themselves.

This is reasserted in the Gospel of St. Thomas, which as noted, is perhaps not only the earliest of the gospels, (55 A.D.?) but also the most authentic.

"Jesus said, If those who lead you say to you, See, the Kingdom is in the sky, then the birds of the sky will proceed you, If they say to you,

It is in the sea, then the fish will proceed you. Rather, the kingdom is inside you, and it is outside of you. When you come to know yourselves, then you will become known, and you will realize that it is you who are the sons of the living Father. But if you will not know yourselves, you dwell in poverty and it is you that are that poverty." (Gospel of St. Thomas #3)

A very logical question at this point, would be to ask what one might find when they go inside themselves. One of the answers to this query, is that one discovers their *true* identity.

ONE'S TRUE IDENTITY

"And the Lord God formed man of the dust of the ground, and breathed into his nostrils the breath of life; and man became a living soul." (Genesis 2:7)

"And so it is written. The first man Adam was made a living soul; The last Adam *was made* a quickening spirit." (I Corinthians 15:45)

Once at a Christmas celebration, this author was chosen to produce and give a trivia quiz to the forty or so persons attending the event. The last question asked was: Who are you? Being unfairly technical, not one individual answered correctly.

Some gave their Christian name, others said "me," or a human being. With their answers, these individuals were identifying with their ego-mind and their human personality. In reality, this is not their true identity; they *are* soul, now, whether they realize it or not.

Not one had answered that they are the "inner man," (Ephesians 3:16) and instead had identified with their ego and mind as themselves, the "earthy man." Some even thought they were their body. This is like a person thinking they are their car, instead of the driver, or that they are their computer, instead of the operator; it is an illusion held by over ninety-nine per cent of the human race. They do not know their true identity. The Christ in Jesus, and Solomon, referred to them as dead.

"But Jesus said unto him, Follow me; and let the dead bury their dead." (Matthew 8:22)

"The man that wandereth out of the way of understanding shall remain in the congregation of the dead." (Proverbs 21:16)

The body, emotions, and mind all perish at death, as "flesh and blood cannot inherit the kingdom of God." (I Corinthians 15:50)

Only the soul, spirit, and divine self of an individual may enter the kingdom of heaven; *this is* one's true identity.

St. Paul states: … "there is a natural body, and there is a spiritual body…, The first man *is* of the earth, earthy: the second man *is* the Lord from heaven." (I Corinthians 15:44-47)

The negative ramifications of thinking that one is their "earthy man," their very thoughts and emotions, are spiritually harmful! Why? Because the mind has been conditioned by the world, and has deeply programmed desires for worldly things: if mind is in control of the individual, and is their governing identity, they are unrealized, and are mired in spiritual illusion.

St. Paul states: "For to be carnally minded *is* death; but to be spiritually minded *is* love and peace. Because the carnal mind *is* enmity against God: for it is not subject to the law of God, neither indeed can be. So then they that are in the flesh cannot please God." (Romans 8:7-8)

A simple example of this mistaken-identity experience, is when people say such and such is good for my soul, or that my soul was stirred by this or that. Those saying such things are identifying with their mind; they have separated themselves from who they really are. They believe that they are the mind and that they have a soul. It is the other way around: they *are* soul and *have* a human mind. The difference is immense as soul and mind are spiritually opposed, and have a totally opposite agenda. In addition, most people are unaware that soul is thousands of times greater than mind, and has existed beyond time.

In the Eastern religions, this mistake, the mind thinking that it is the soul, is called *maya* or illusion (Rama). It is a rare individual on earth that has seen through this illusion.

Others believe that soul and mind are the same thing, and that their mind's thoughts are who they are as soul. That is untrue as the two could not be more separate. Notice that in the great commandment they are separated as completely different things:

"Jesus said unto him, Thou shall love the Lord thy God with all thy heart, and with all thy soul, and with all thy mind." (Matthew 22:37)

In addition, the fact that one can completely change and subjugate their own mind, proves that one is *not* the mind, but the *force* subjugating the mind, the soul, one's true self. Those being run by their mind are not going to subjugate mind, as that would mean Satan casting out Satan, (Matthew 12:26) or like choosing Mrs. Fox (mind) to guard the chicken coop (mind). Ms. Fox has a large litter of kits to feed, (worldly desires) and is not going to let them or herself go hungry.

Christ must take over the individual, and transform the carnal mind into a spiritual mind. The mind cannot, and will not, do this; in the beginning of one's spiritual journey, the mind will cunningly fight soul, and Christ, to keep its priorities and desires intact. The secret teachings believe that it is one's own mind that is Satan, and that the concept of a so-called devil is merely a cover, for those who are unwilling to accept responsibility for their own evil. There is *no* force opposing God but the unrealized individual.

It may be helpful at this point to define soul, as many people have difficulty in identifying what it is. They often have little trouble in separating their emotions from the mind, but struggle to separate mind from soul. This mistake is easy to make, as one's mind is a reflection of one's soul, and similar to it, but in a much scaled down way.

There are two *main* consciousness' in man, the mind and the soul, the soul being completely independent of the mind's activity, and their perspective and point of view are often opposite to each other. The mind and ego are one's thoughts, and the center of one's I-ness in the human consciousness.

Soul, one's true self, is a completely separate consciousness, and not accessible by the mind; it is a center of consciousness much deeper inside oneself; it is linked to one's intuition, conscience, hunches, and feeling of themselves, their deeper *I-ness*. It is one's gut, the source of one's intuition, that voice in the back of the head, that one might hear now and then, especially with warnings; it is that feeling of what is right or wrong, and how one *feels* like themselves. Soul is one's deeper, innate *"I-ness,"* and it is always there, even when the mind is totally blank. *It is the deeper you.*

In the Holy Bible, sometimes soul is called an angel or angel-like, as when the disciples tell Rhoda that she has seen Peter's angel at the door, and not the flesh and blood Peter whom they thought was in prison, (Acts 12:15) or when the Christ in Jesus tells the disciples that the children's angels (souls) are in heaven, and "do always behold the face of my father." (Matthew 18:10)

Soul permeates the mind and personality, much as smoke may permeate the air of a room, even though smoke and air are two separate things. This can make separating the two difficult as they share a reflective likeness, and have the same *feeling* of oneself.

However, soul is much greater than the mind, having existed eternally; it has a much greater awareness and consciousness, so great that it cannot be measured; its memory of all it has learned through countless lives is its understanding, which also determines which rung has been reached on Jacob's ladder, or which of the seven heavens soul has reached. Souls are measured by their level of understanding and awareness, not their intelligence.

As noted, one's deep feeling of themselves as to who they are, permeates the personality, and is present even when the mind is still. If by the grace of God, one is given a conscious out-of-body experience, as St. Paul was in II Corinthians 12:1-2, when he is caught up into the third heaven, one in their soul form "feels" no differently than when in the body, and even though they are without their earthly personality and mind, they still *feel* like themselves.

This feeling of oneself, their genuine I-ness, is perhaps the easiest way in which to identify one's own true self while in the human body, since it is always there. This has absolutely nothing to do with the emotions, and those thinking that their emotional body is soul are dwelling in illusion.

The fact that this feeling of oneself *is soul*, makes death of the body seem like a virtual nothing, as many do not notice any change in their feeling of who they are when they pass, and since they are still conscious, ask others if they have died. It is as though one has stepped out of their car, the car being the mind, emotions and body.

Soul survives death of the body and has been existent forever. If realized, soul has tremendous powers that are difficult to believe. For example, it can project itself anywhere in the universe, or run multiple bodies in different dimensions. It has tremendous wisdom, and knows everything on its level of heaven and below.

Some of its powers were demonstrated by the disciples of Christ, when for example, they healed the sick, or when Philip helped the people of Samaria believe by performing miracles, (Acts 8:6) or disappears into thin air after baptizing a eunuch, (Acts 8:39) or when Peter raises Tabitha from the dead. (Acts 9:36-41)

Of course, this pales beside what Christ through Jesus demonstrated! The Eastern religions teach that at the level of the fifth heaven, soul's aura has the radiance of sixteen suns. Believers glimpsing their *own* luminous body at death, or in a near death experience, often believe it is Jesus, or God.

The mind and ego do not survive death, and are only interested in caring for the body's needs and desires. When soul incarnates into a new body on Earth, it receives a new lower mind body, emotional body, lunar body, and physical body. This makes it very difficult to remember one's past lives, but provides an entirely fresh start for one's spiritual journey, and the continued climb on Jacob's ladder. The human consciousness would be instantly fused if it remembered its past lives.

The secret teachings believe, that it is possible for the human consciousness to form a close relationship with soul through daily devotions, combined with living a Christ-like life, and that one may increase their communication with soul through prayer, intuition, visions, dreams, flashes, signs, and communion with the Word.

This eventually leads to the human consciousness blending with soul, and adopting it as one's true identity and point of view. In other words, one has not only accepted Christ, one has conformed themselves to Christ, and realized that they are a "Lord from heaven." The Lords of heaven attempt to view everything through Christ's eyes.

"The first man *is* of the earth, earthy: the second man *is* the Lord from heaven." (I Corinthians 15:47)

Concurrent with this merging with soul is a withdrawing from worldly identifications, and a total surrender of the individual's mind and ego to the Christ within, as Christ, through one's own spirit and soul, takes over one's life. This step, often called "being born of the spirit," allows soul's entry into the kingdom of heaven, and the first level of the Christ Consciousness; this profound viewpoint is a wonder of acute perception and knowingness, occurring in the innermost part of one's consciousness.

This experience is a life-changing event and very exalted, for suddenly one is looking through deeper eyes, a complete turnaround from the personality's point of view, and everything is seen in a wonderful new light.

"Therefore, if any man *be* in Christ, *he is* a new creature: old things are passed away; behold, all things are become new." (II Corinthians 5:17)

This is called self-realization in the Eastern religions, when one has realized they are soul, and have become one with it. The secret doctrine calls this salvation, or being born of the spirit, something the Christ in Jesus says must happen to enter the kingdom of heaven.

"Jesus answered, Verily, verily, I say unto thee, Except a man be born of water and *of* the Spirit, he cannot enter into the kingdom of God." (John 3:5)

One of the differences between mainstream Christianity and the hidden teachings, is that the esoteric doctrine examines the entire process of soul's growth, from before and after soul's present incarnation. This process is aptly illustrated in the Christian Bible by two allegories in the book of Genesis, the first being the creation account, and the second being Jacob's dream of the ladder of heaven. Perhaps these two allegories answer the questions of why soul is on Earth in the first place, and the overall process of soul's growth in eternity.

THE PROCESS OF SOUL'S GROWTH

The creation allegory in the book of Genesis, gives one important clues as to why soul is down on earth, and what it must do to return to heaven. According to the hidden doctrine, there are, for simple explanative purposes, two kinds of souls in heaven, innocent, and realized.

There are those that have eaten from the tree of the knowledge of good and evil, and have then returned to heaven; there are also those that have not left heaven yet, and have not eaten of the tree. Adam and Eve were innocent and unrealized, living blissfully in the garden of heaven, symbolized by the fact they were not even conscious that they were naked.

"And they were both naked, the man and his wife, and were not ashamed." (Genesis 2:25)

In addition, they were naïve as to what good and evil were, as they had not yet eaten from the tree of the knowledge of good and evil. This abruptly changes when Eve is enticed by the serpent to eat from the tree, and subsequently, shares the fruit with Adam. Esoteric teachings do not believe in the concept of a devil or Satanic being, and view the serpent as another aspect of God, enticing Adam and Eve to leave heaven, and eventually become realized beings.

Of course, God knows what they will do. Notice that what the Lord God "tells" Adam and Eve will happen if they eat from the tree, does not happen.

"God hath said, Ye shall not eat of it, neither shall ye touch it, lest ye die." (Genesis 3:3)

What the "Serpent" tells them will occur does happen. "And the serpent said unto the woman, Ye shall not surely die: For God doth know that in the day ye eat thereof, then your eyes shall be opened, and ye shall be as Gods, knowing good and evil." (Genesis 3:4-5) Subsequently, what the serpent has told them is confirmed by God:

"And the Lord God said, Behold, the man is become as one of us, to know good and evil: and now, lest he put forth his hand, and take also of the tree of life, and eat, and live forever: Therefore the Lord God sent him forth from the garden of Eden, to till the ground from whence he was taken." (Genesis 23:2-3)

What is said by both the serpent and the Lord God is confirmed. As soon as Eve and Adam eat from the tree, their eyes are opened, and they immediately lose their innocence; their first perception of evil has occurred.

"And the eyes of them both were opened, and they knew that they were naked; and they sewed fig leaves together, and made themselves aprons." (Genesis 3:7)

Adam and Eve have begun their long journey in the lower heavens, and the Lord God tells them of what they will endure.

"Unto the woman he said, I will greatly multiply thy sorrow and thy conception; in sorrow thou shall bring forth children; and thy desire *shall be* to thy husband, and he shall rule over thee. And onto Adam he said, Because thou has hearkened unto the voice of thy wife, and hast eaten from the tree, of which I commanded thee, saying, Thou shall not eat of it: cursed *is* the ground for thy sake; in sorrow shalt thou eat *of* it all the days of thy life; Thorns also and thistles shall it bring forth to thee; and thou shalt eat the herb of the field; In the sweat of thy face shalt thou eat bread, till thou return unto the ground; for out of it wast thou taken: for dust thou *art*, and unto dust shalt thou return." (Genesis 3:16-19)

The Adam and Eve allegory has been interpreted in many different ways, especially as to what the main players symbolize; however, perhaps it fair to say that there is a central theme or point: Adam and Eve have been tempted, enticed, or sent to dwell in the worlds below from the heaven worlds above, where the quest for realization, salvation, and immortality will begin. It will be a long and arduous journey before being allowed to reenter the garden and eat from the tree of life. And when they do, they will no longer be innocent and unrealized: they will realize what good and evil are, and why Christ is the ultimate good.

This allegory offers insight into what God's plan is for soul, and why humanity has been subjected to lifetimes in this world of pain and sorrow. It is up to each individual soul to learn and discern what evil consists of, subsequently embracing the good, the true, and the beautiful: Christ. They will achieve realization, salvation, immortality, and unspeakable love, wisdom, power, and freedom; they will live in ecstasy.

A second allegory in Genesis, Jacob's dream of the ladder of heaven, amplifies and reinforces information of God's plan, as revealed by the account of Adam and Eve.

"And Jacob went out from Beersheba, and went toward Haran. And he lighted upon a certain place, and tarried there all night, because the sun was set; and he took of the stones of that place, and put *them for* his pillows, and lay down in that place to sleep. And he dreamed, and behold a ladder set up on the earth, and the top of it reached to heaven: and behold the angels of God ascending and descending on it. And, behold, the Lord stood above it, …." (Genesis 28:10-13)

"And Jacob awaked out of his sleep, and he said, Surely the Lord is in this place; and I knew *it* not. And he was afraid, and said, How dreadful *is* this place! This *is* none other than the house of God, and this *is* the gate of heaven." (Genesis 28:16-17)

There are several important revelations in this allegory: the first is that there *is* a metaphorical ladder of heaven, on which angels (souls) are ascending and descending; this is similar to Adam and Eve descending from heaven, and having to begin their ascension back towards heaven.

In addition, Jacob calls this the "gate of heaven," which reinforces the premise that this *is* the process in place, for souls leaving and returning to heaven. Additional confirmation comes when Jacob states that this dream has revealed to him "God's house," and he names the place *Bethel*, house of God. (Genesis 28:19)

These two allegories provide a brief overview of the entire process of God's plan for souls, and why they have been enticed to descend from heaven, and eventually, ascend back as realized souls to be with the Lord.

Christ taught that there were many mansions in His Father's house, (John 14:2) which equates to many rungs on the ladder of heaven, and they are often divided into seven dimensions or heavens.

There are many different charts of these heavens by differing religions and paths, and while the names of the regions differ in competing religions, there are not any differences concerning the heavens' order, characteristics, and purpose.

Contrary to what Western believers might think, there are thousands of volumes written about the seven heavens, especially in the East, and increasingly in the West, as many saints and teachers from the past, and present, have visited these heavens in dreams, experiences as soul, and visions from the Lord.

Each level of heaven represents a "grade" in God's school for souls, as they learn and evolve into spiritual beings, fit for the return to the top of God's house. This will make them sons of God, and fulfil Christ's promise in the book of John.

"But as many received him, he gave power to become sons of God, *even* to them that believe on his name." (John 1:12) The word "become" in this wonderful promise, supports an important distinction about salvation: those that have received Christ are *not* sons of God yet, but have been given power to *become* sons of God.

A *very* brief overview of the seven heavens will be presented next, before describing each heaven individually. Voluminous texts describing these heavens can be found in Hinduism, Sufism, Buddhism, Sikhism, Christian Theosophy, the Rosicrucian's, the Sant Mat teachings of Northern India, light and sound paths such as Masterpath, *Radha Soami, Ruhani Satsang,* and Eckankar. While some paths may divide the heavens in different places, they are *all* strikingly uniform. It is also fair to say that this knowledge has been around for many thousands of years.

The object here, other than a general description, is to dwell on what soul is learning on the *subjective side* of these heavens, rather than presenting endless details of what exists on the *objective side* of the heavens. Before describing the individual heavens, a brief synopsis of aspects and characteristics concerning the entire creation will proceed; this will be a compendium without apparent organization. This information is an amalgam of deeper Christly teachings from all over the globe, and personal accounts by saints, disciples, and the Christ in Jesus.

THE SEVEN HEAVENS OF CREATION

*   At the very center of creation, the Word broadcasts forth in all directions from a center within the heart of God, similar to a radio station's transmitter. God continually sends forth ITS wondrous spirit to the furthest reaches of creation, and once arriving there, the Holy Word travels back to the center, much as the heart pumps blood to the furthest reaches of the body, and then receives it back through the veins to its original beginning point; the Holy Spirit has both a centrifugal and centripetal action.

"All the rivers run into the sea; yet the sea is not full; unto the place from whence the rivers come, thither they return again." (Ecclesiastics 1:7)

*   As the Word travels out from the center, it gradually diminishes in vibration, and in doing so, creates differing dimensions which make up the seven heavens. This means that the heavens go *in*, and not *up:* as a result, going to a higher heaven means going inside to a higher vibrational dimension, which is invisible to human senses.
*   The Christ in Jesus affirms this in Luke 17:20-21. "And when he was demanded of the Pharisee's, when the kingdom of God should come, he answered them and said, The Kingdom of God cometh not with observation; Neither shall they say, Lo here! Or, lo there! for, behold, the kingdom of God is within you."
*   The creation appears as a multi-dimensional, polarized ovoid. It is very positive at the top, neutral in the center, and very negative at

the bottom. The planet Earth is in the first (lowest) heaven, and is very close to the negative pole.

* All of the seven heavens are often divided into seven sublevels; these are each divided into seven sub planes, and each of those are further divided by seven. This diminution by sevens continues.
* The top three heavens, five, six, and seven, are purely positive and are never destroyed. The souls residing there are angel-like, deathless, and live in total joy. (Luke 20:36)

This *is* the Garden of Eden. There are souls here similar to Adam and Eve, in that they are unrealized, and are descending Jacob's ladder; there are also realized souls here on their way up the ladder.

"But they which shall be accounted worthy to obtain that world, and the resurrection from the dead, neither marry nor are given in marriage: Neither can they die anymore: for they are equal unto the angels; and are the children of God, being the children of the resurrection." (Luke 20:35-36)

* The lower four heavens are dual, as the Word divides into two major streams at the top of the fourth heaven. Everything in these lower four heavens has an opposite: day/night, light/dark, life/death, young/old, good/evil. These levels are considered a training ground for soul. They are kept perfectly balanced, and the tension between the two opposing forces produces creation.
* The bottom four heavens are periodically destroyed and recreated, and offer an infinite number of states and experiences for soul to experience while climbing Jacob's ladder. The book of Hebrews affirms this cycle.

"You Lord, did lay the foundation of the earth in the beginning, and the heavens are the works of your hands. They will perish but You remain *and* continue permanently; they will all wear out like a garment. Like a mantle You will roll them up, and they will be changed *and* replaced by others…." (Hebrews 1:10-12 Amplified King James)

* The lower four heavens are allegorically represented in the Holy Bible by the tree of the knowledge of good and evil. The dual

energies that run these lower heavens are often called the positive and negative forces, or the Yang and the Yin. Some religions, worship deities representing the positive side of the dual forces, as God; many religions have termed the negative part of these forces Satan, evil, or dark, not realizing that these energies are also the Holy Spirit; they are divine and purposeful. The Almighty, and the kingdom of God, are *above* both the positive and negative forces.

"Let every soul be subject unto the higher powers. For there is no power but of God: the powers that be are ordained of God." (Romans 13:1)

*   The negative forces match the positive forces and help keep the lower heavens in perfect balance; they also help teach soul what good and evil are, as the results of sinful actions bring unpleasant returns to those who commit them, and souls soon realize that it is their own creation coming back to their source. There is no devil or Satan needed in creation; evil comes from man and his desires, not from God.

"Let no man say when he is tempted, I am tempted of God: for God cannot be tempted with evil, neither tempteth any man: But every man is tempted, when he is drawn away of his own lust, and enticed. Then when lust hath conceived, it bringeth forth sin: and sin, when it is finished, bringeth forth death." (James 1:13-15)

"Be not deceived; God is not mocked; for whatsoever a man soweth, that shall he also reap. For he that soweth to his flesh shall of the flesh reap corruption; but he that soweth to the spirit shall of the spirit reap life everlasting." (Galatians 6:7-8)

"For we must all appear before the judgement seat of Christ; that everyone may receive the things *done* in his body, according to that he hath done, whether *it be* good or bad." (II Corinthians 5:10)

"But I say unto you, That every idle word that men shall speak, they shall give account thereof in the day of judgement." (John 12:36)

The deeper teachings believe that Christ forgives and welcomes those who sincerely accept Him, in the sense that He does not deny accepting a soul for previous sinful behavior; however, the Holy Bible teaches that they will reap what they have sown, and their suffering will be the instrument of their learning, and the cross that they must bear as they are crucified with Christ. (Romans 6:6)

* Time and space exist in the lower four heavens, but the highest three heavens are formless and without time and space; they are separated by differing vibrational levels and states of consciousness. This means that soul can travel in the lower heavens from place to place, or heaven to heaven, but in the higher heavens this is not possible; instead, soul projects itself into these regions by going inside, or outside.
* Since the levels of heaven go increasingly "in" as one goes higher, one effect of this is that all of the heavens are "right here in the room with us." As marvelous as it may seem, one can travel to any level of heaven without moving the body an inch, simply by switching one's consciousness to their own appropriate consciousness-center (body) that exists at that level, or by simply projecting there as soul.
* It is perfectly normal for advanced souls to travel within their physical bodies while sleeping, and visit various levels of heaven. Advanced souls under Christ's direction may learn to travel outside of themselves. How high a soul may travel into the heavens at night depends on the soul's evolvement, or position on Jacob's ladder. Most of the souls traveling at night are visiting the second level of heaven, commonly called the Astral Plane, and are usually studying and learning. Many are also helping other souls in various ways.

"O Lord, the God of my salvation, I have cried to you for help by day; at night I am in Your presence." (Psalm 88:1) (Amplified King James)

Numerous mystical saints, such as St. Theresa de Avila, Padre Pio, St. John of the Cross, and St. Francis de Assisi, are famous in part for their out-of-body travels, and many religious believers claim to have met them in inner experiences, visions and dreams. Millions of Christians also claim to have had, and are having, experiences with

Christ. Millions of sincere followers in other religions have also had such experiences. Christ is omnipresent.

"In a dream, in a vision of the night, when deep sleep falleth upon men, in slumbering's upon the bed; Then he openeth the ears of men, and sealeth their instruction, that he may withdraw man *from his* purpose, and hide pride from man." (Job 33:15)

* It is because man was created in the image of God, that man's being is a perfect microcosm of the creation; one effect of this, is that the levels of heaven are inside and outside the body.

As the Christ in Jesus states: …" Rather the kingdom is inside you, and it is outside you…." (Gospel of St. Thomas #3)

In addition, Christ Jesus offers clarity in Luke 17:20-21: "And when he was demanded of the Pharisees, when the kingdom of God should come, he answered them and said, The kingdom of God cometh not with observation: Neither shall they say lo here! or, lo there! for, behold, the kingdom of God is within you."

St. Paul reveals this inner kingdom (presumably his own) in an aside, in II Corinthians 12:2-4: "I knew a man in Christ above fourteen years ago, (whether in the body, I cannot tell; or whether out of the body, I cannot tell: God knoweth;) such an one caught up to the third heaven. And I knew such a man, (whether in the body or out of the body, I cannot tell: God knoweth;) How that he was caught up into paradise, and heard unspeakable words, which it is not lawful for a man to utter." (II Corinthians 12:2-4)

* Soul has a consciousness or body on each of the levels of heaven within one which it inhabits, just as it inhabits one's human body in the first heaven. Inside the physical body is a finer body called the lunar body, which is a perfect template of the physical body, but at a higher vibration. It distributes energy from above, (within) and has much to do with the formation, growth, and maintenance of the physical body.

On the second level of heaven, often called the Astral Plane, soul has an astral body containing the emotional consciousness; sometimes it is called the desire body, as this is the source of desire and passion, good and bad.

Soul maintains a lower mental body on the lower four sublevels of the third heaven, called the lower Mental Plane: it is the seat of concrete thought, the senses, and other aspects of the lower mind.

On the top three sublevels of the third heaven, often called the Causal Plane, (*Brahm*) is a sheath dealing with abstract thought, and the seeds of causes and karmic patterns from soul's uncountable lifetimes.

In the fourth heaven, often called the High Mental Plane, (*Buddhic Plane, Par Brahm*) soul has a higher mind sheath that is intuitive, and closely connected to soul. It is used for discernment and making fine distinctions. Soul also maintains a thin sheath at the top of this heaven containing the unconscious (*Saguna Brahm*).

So far, these bodies mentioned are the lower four heavens' vehicles, and are simply like space suits that soul uses for protection, when incarnating into the lower dual heavens.

In the higher three heavens, soul has a soul body *(atma)*) it uses in the fifth heaven, called the Soul Plane, a spirit self on the sixth level of heaven called the high soul, (monad, *atman*) and finally, at the very core of one's being, a divine self, or Christ Self, (*PARAM atman*) on the seventh level of heaven (Brahman).

This perfectly reflects the spiritual hierarchy that runs the entire seven heavens of God. This also explains *how* man is created in God's image. Soul, as a cell of the body of Christ, is a perfect replica and microcosm of Christ's creation.

"Jesus answered them, Is it not written in your law, I said, Ye are Gods?" (John 10:34)

*   In the secret teachings, soul is divided into a low soul and a high soul. The high soul, called atman in Eastern religions, or the monad in Western thought, stays in the sixth heaven at all times. The Christ in Jesus makes this point when calling a child to Him, and then setting him in the midst of the disciples.

"Take heed that ye despise not one of these little ones; for I say unto you, That in heaven their angels [souls] do always behold the face of my Father which is in heaven." (Matthew 18:10)

- * The low soul, (also called the ego in some Western disciplines) is called the *jiva* in Eastern religions, and is atoms of the high soul (monad or atman) projected down into the lower heavens for experience (Adam and Eve); this consciousness resides in the fifth, fourth, and third plane bodies (soul body, high mental body, causal body); the human soul, a reflection of the low soul, resides in the low mental, astral, and physical bodies.

These divisions or stations have some relevance and convenience when discussing soul's growth. For simplification, the terms low soul and high soul will be used when referring to these two main divisions of soul.

- * In all cases, it is wise to remember that soul is the consciousness *inside* these bodies; soul is *not* these protective sheaths; it is operating them and attempting to make them amenable to its will.
- * It is the low soul and its human reflection that Christ redeems and saves. The high soul *has* been saved already, so to speak: it has already completed the journey into the lower dual planes and back: it is in heaven permanently. Only the low soul and its reflective human soul need purifying. The Christ in Jesus makes this point through metaphor to Simon Peter, when washing the feet of His disciples.

"Peter saith unto him, Thou shalt never wash my feet. Jesus answered him, If I wash thee not, thou hast no part with me. Simon Peter saith unto him, Lord, not my feet only, but also *my* hands and *my* head. Jesus saith unto him, He that is washed needeth not save to wash *his* feet, but is clean every whit: and ye are clean but not all." (John 13:9-10)

- * The divine self, projects atoms of its consciousness into these bodies that are scaled down in size and power, the further out from the source they go, but it is always the same self. In all of these bodies, one *is* soul, spirit, and the divine self. The main difference between these bodies, is in the *amount* of itself soul has in each.

* It is the low soul, with its human reflection, that is the true prodigal son. Admittedly, this can be confusing, since often times the low soul and the high soul are both called the higher self, and relative to the human consciousness, they both qualify as "higher selves"; none the less, only the low soul needs redeeming. It *is* the lost sheep.
* These bodies are often called sheaths, and they protect soul and spirit from the coarse vibrations of the lower four heavens. As soul climbs Jacob's ladder, gradually progressing to higher and higher heavens, it drops the bodies it no longer needs, just as it vacates the human body at its end.
* It is important to note that the deeper teachings stress divine guidance by Christ and His channels in all of the heavens. It is considered profitable to get help from some soul which has completed the journey back to at least the fifth heaven, which is the beginning of the kingdom of God. At the start of one's spiritual journey, after one has accepted Christ as one's guide and savior, the Holy Word may lead the student to a disciple/teacher that is spiritually qualified, and can help the student get started.

This is a practice that many utilize, but it is an option, not a requirement; if desired, one can always go it alone, and going it alone, is what it will ultimately come to in everyone's future. The ideal is to meet Christ *inside* oneself. This is also true for any disciple/teacher representing Christ.

As one grows in Christ, one will increasingly rely on their own divine guidance from their own higher soul, which is in much closer communion with Christ than one's human consciousness. One of the primary goals for the low soul, and its human counterpart, is to become self-directed through guidance from the Christ within. This is termed "being one's own priest" in the Old Testament.

"But the anointing ye have received of him abideth in you, and ye need not that any man teach you: but as the same anointing teacheth you of all things, and is truth, and is no lie, and even as it hath taught you, ye shall abide in him." (I John 2:27)

* It is difficult to impart soul's experience to the human brain, which has a very limited capacity compared to soul's vast consciousness. It may be compared to communicating with one's pet. St. Paul is not exaggerating when calling one's spiritual body "the Lord of heaven." (I Corinthians 15:47)

The Christ in Jesus, quoting the Old Testament, (Psalm 82:6) declared outright that "[we] are God's." (John 10:34)

* Each of the lower four, dual heavens have an objective and subjective side: an inner finer dimension, and an outer grosser dimension. The subjective side is slightly inside the objective side in vibration, and therefore at the "top" of the plane. It is more positive and spiritual in nature; it is often called the inner side of the outer plane. It is this book's aim to dwell primarily on what soul experiences on the subjective, more spiritual side of these heavens. The objective characteristics of the heavens are infinite.
* Each heaven increases tremendously in size as one goes in, and the further in one goes, the more souls there are living in these paradises. The highest heaven of manifest creation, the seventh, is by far the largest and circumscribes all the rest; this plane also has by far the most souls (spirits) residing there, as this process of souls climbing Jacob's ladder to the top has been ongoing eternally. These spirt-souls have become their Christ-Self, their divine self. They have claimed their divine inheritance as "heirs of God and joint heirs with Christ." (Romans 8:17)
* These spirit-souls make up an infinite ocean of love, mercy, wisdom, power, and freedom in the highest heaven of creation. This *is* the Christ Consciousness, the highest consciousness of the Word in creation, and every soul/spirit there is a participating drop of that infinite, incomprehensible ocean. This unfathomable sea of love is the Christ, the Son/Daughter of God. Joining that indescribable consciousness, is the infinite dream of all creation.

"But as many as received him, to them gave he power to become the sons of God, *even* to them that believe on his name: which were born, not of blood, nor of the will of the flesh, nor of the will of man, but of God." (John 1:12-13)

*   One of the central pillars of the secret teachings, is that the Holy Spirit can be heard with the inner ears in all of the seven heavens. This is unknown in mainstream Christianity, but well-known in the secret teachings, and other world religions. Recognition of this practice is rapidly growing in the West, in part because of the spread of Eastern teachings, and also from the fact that millions of people are experiencing it.

Many adherents of the hidden secrets, believe that listening to the sounds of the Word inside oneself, is the quintessential devotional practice. Many listen to the Holy Spirit to stop thinking and practice stillness. This has absolutely nothing to do with the physical ears.

And what does one hear? The sounds are very high, continuous, and very faint, perhaps like ringing chimes at a distance; others describe it as the sound that high electrical wires emit occasionally, or as a ringing in the ears. One may hear multiple streams of sound, and often times, these faint melodies are so much a part of one's innate background sound, that it usually takes stillness and concentrated focus to hear them.

This has nothing to do with tinnitus, which is comprised of loud, lower, grating noises caused by a medical problem, or perhaps a consciousness condition; those sounds can be very annoying and torture millions. Many have received relief from tinnitus by elevating their consciousness.

These beautiful sounds of the Word are often symbolized in spiritual literature as a flute, lute, harp, bell, reed, pipe, chime, vina, or some other high-pitched instrument. An example would be Rumi's, *Song of the Reed*. These melodies are often referred to as the music of the universe, or the voice of God: these high frequencies are often imitated with highly pitched string instruments, or with tinkling bells, chimes and ringing bowls.

The streams of sound produced by the Holy Word are very soft, soothing, and calming, and they may be difficult to hear in the beginning. Some have had the experience of hearing multitudes of sounds akin to beautiful orchestral music. This ineffable river of joy is also called the fountain of God, or the song of the Lord. Christ in Jesus speaks of those able to hear his voice, which the secret teaching interprets as the audible Holy Word.

"My sheep know my voice, and I know them, and they follow me: And I give unto them eternal life; and they shall never perish, neither shall any man pluck them out of my hand." (John 10: 27-28)

"Blessed *is* the people that know the joyful sound: they shall walk, O Lord, in the light of thy countenance." (Psalms 89:15)

These celestial notes are the Word passing through the energy centers (*chakras*) of one's bodies, and doing the work of sustaining every aspect of one's being. This wondrous euphony of sound is referred to in the Holy Scriptures as a "still, small voice"; perhaps, this is a confirmation of its subtleness and faintness." (I Kings 19:12)

Ezekiel and St. John, also refer to the Son of man's voice as "the sounds of many waters"; perhaps, this is referring to the rich symphony of sounds one may hear. (Ezekiel 43:2) (Revelation 1:15)

"And in the midst of the seven candlesticks *one* like unto the Son of man, clothed with a garment down to the foot, and girt about the paps with a golden girdle. His head and *his* hairs were white as wool, as white as snow; and his eyes *were* as a flame of fire; And his feet like unto fine brass, as if they burned in a furnace; and his voice as the sound of many waters." (Revelation 1:13-16)

The beautiful simile that St. John uses to describe the Son of man's voice, accurately depicts the complexity of what one may hear. Ten of the most major sounds, out of thousands, are said to come from the seven heavens, five from the purely positive planes, and five from the lower dual levels.

Generally, the higher the sounds, the higher the level of heaven. Soul can learn to travel on these streams of sound, as everything in creation is inter-connected by the Word. At the base of one's being, where the Holy Word first enters the individual, is a roaring waterfall of uncountable frequencies, dispersing to complete myriads of missions within the human body. Soul rides the centripetal motion of these divine streams, which are returning to their Source, to higher and higher heavens.

The Christ in Jesus, through metaphor, compares the Holy Spirit to the wind, and states that those born of the Spirit, can hear the Spirit.

"The wind bloweth where it listeth, and thou hearest the sound thereof, but canst not tell whence it cometh, and whither it goeth: so is everyone that is born of the Spirit." (John 3:8)

"Verily, verily, I say unto you, The hour is coming, and now is, when the dead shall hear the voice of the Son of God: and they that hear shall live." (John 5:25)

According to the protected teachings, the fact that the Holy Current is inwardly audible is extremely important. One aspect of this importance is that for advanced students under Christ, soul can use these sounds to communicate with the human consciousness: this is done by soul markedly increasing the volume at precisely particular moments, and usually for just a few seconds.

It may be a warning just before a contemplated action; it may be a confirmation of a specific thought; it may protest a particular thought; it may be knowledge of something upcoming; it may point one to a kindred soul; it may be a signal to remain alert; it may be information available to intuition; it may suddenly come on louder for any number of reasons.

This is not something that happens frequently, and instances of when it does come on significantly louder are usually auspicious, and often precious. Information is gleaned in the present moment that is unavailable by conventional means. Those high souls enjoying this communicative relationship with soul, can point to dozens of experiences where these audible directives changed their lives, not only in little ways, but in major ways beyond the imagination's reach.

These messages are interpreted intuitively; usually, one instantly knows what is being shared; sometimes, one finds out later; at other times, although rare, one is left wondering what was communicated. This system of communication is of great importance, because it is a means of direct and immediate messaging from the high soul, to the human soul and physical consciousness.

The spiritual help that one may be given via this avenue is incalculable. It also leads to being born of the spirit, as the deeper teachings propose that this relationship with the audible Word, is necessary to enter the kingdom of God. As noted: the Christ in Jesus states in John 3:8, that one born of the spirit, can hear the spirit, like people hear the wind.

* Upon death of the body, souls do not all go to the same heaven, but go to the heaven they have earned. Souls vary in spiritual progress, and their vibration rate must match the heaven they go to, whether it be a level of hell, the very top of the seventh heaven, or some level in between these two.

"*There is* one glory of the sun, and another of the moon, and another glory of the stars: for *one* star [soul] differeth from *another* star in glory." (I Corinthians 15:41)

* What distinguishes one soul (and person) from another in evolution, is their level of *realization* and *awareness,* not their intelligence. While there is a correlation between having a fine mind, and one's attained rung on Jacob's ladder, it is limited. For example, very intelligent persons have been known to be dictators, hunt for sport, or engage in power plays, violence, theft, murder, rape, lying, cheating, etcetera. An *aware* or *realized* person would do none of these things. The level of awareness and realization achieved, is soul's intelligence quotient, and indicates the heaven of their residence.
* The overwhelming majority of souls in this "generation," as the Christ in Jesus called them, are working from the second heaven; perhaps ten per cent are from the third heaven; less than one per cent are from the fourth heaven; those from the fifth heaven and higher are one in many million. Uncountable generations have gone before this present one; uncountable generations are coming after this one: forever.

Mankind today is the same generation that was on Earth in Jesus' time, and continually reincarnates as the age progresses. Christ Jesus directly points this out, when He foretells the end of this age.

"But in those days, after that tribulation, the sun shall be darkened, and the moon shall not give her light, And the stars of heaven shall fall, and the powers that are in heaven shall be shaken. Verily I say unto you, that this generation shall not pass, till all these things be done." (Mark 13:24-25,30)

Each of the levels of heaven is a scaled down reflection of the one above it, and although at a lower vibration, reflects the one above it in every detail that is strong enough to manifest. Telephones are a reflection of telepathy on a higher level. Airplanes are a reflection of flying saucers on higher levels, which are a reflection of flying without aids, and flying like Superman is a step-down from instant projection.

In the same way, the Christ Consciousness reflects downward through the heavens in steps, as awareness, knowingness, intuition, intelligence, instinct, and emotion.

* The secret teachings of Christ that describe the seven heavens, are the same in all religions and paths, be it in Christianity, Judaism, Hinduism, Buddhism, Islam, Sikhism, Jainism, Taoism, Tantra, Shintoism, Theosophy, American Indian beliefs, and many others. One cannot divorce Christ from any person, path or religion, as Christ is at the heart of it.

A primary reason for this harmony between deeper teachings, is that advanced disciples, saints, monks, and others deep in Christ, all find the same things when journeying into the heaven worlds through visions and dreams. These evolved souls in Christ are the spiritual torchbearers for mankind.

"Then Peter opened *his* mouth, and said, of a truth I perceive that God is no respecter of persons: But in every nation he that feareth him, and worketh righteousness, is accepted with him." (Acts 10:34-35)

This universality of truth is expressed in the East as follows: "Ekam sat vipra bahudha vadanti." "That which exists is one; sages call it by various names."

The Holy Bible states the same principle as follows: "Hear, O Israel: The Lord our God *is* one Lord: ...." (Deuteronomy 6:4)

* Soul's growth throughout eternity is incredibly slow, by human standards. Soul has lived forever beyond all time, and it is difficult to teach new things to a soul that has been growing and evolving for eternity. Anything that could be learned quickly would already

have been learned; in addition, souls in the higher heavens are so happy, that there is little incentive to progress further. Lifetimes on Earth and similar planets are a matter of minutes to soul.

*   The secret doctrine believes that soul, as an atom of Christ, begins its journey from the highest heaven, progressively descending step by step to the fifth heaven. It is ignorant of who it is, and what it can potentially do. After a thorough preparation, it successively descends through the elemental kingdoms, before beginning its ascension through the mineral kingdom, the plant kingdom, the animal kingdom, and man.

The highest souls of the animal kingdom, present within domestic pets and animals interrelating with man, will comprise the next "generation"; this is very far in the future.

*   Souls in a human body, whatever level of development they have achieved, are relatively, incredibly evolved. Further spiritual growth means gradually ascending the levels of heaven, eventually arriving back at the original starting place as a realized soul, a soul that can operate with full awareness and control, throughout the seven heavens as a co-laborer with Christ. There are zillions of job openings in helping Christ maintain Creation.

"For we are labourers together with God; ye are God's husbandry, *ye are* God's building." (I Corinthians 3:9)

*   Soul is not saved in one glorious moment, but attains salvation after long cycles of growth. In addition, there are long transition periods between levels of heaven, as profound, new, higher consciousness's must be learned and adopted. Soul must learn how to survive in a level of heaven, whether it be on Earth in the first heaven, or some higher level that will contain new challenges and a required higher consciousness.

"Wherefore, my beloved, as ye have always obeyed, not as in my presence only, but now much more in my absence, work out your own salvation with fear and trembling." (Philippians 2:12)

"And no man hath ascended up to heaven, but he that came down from heaven, *even* the Son of man which is in heaven." (John 3:13)

* There is a point in Soul's development where the slow pace of growth changes noticeably. When soul accepts Christ as its guide and savior, immense changes occur, and as soul and the human consciousness begin to conform themselves to Christ, growth accelerates. One is now cooperating with Christ and His spiritual principles, instead of one's lower, carnal desires. The believer is beginning to realize their very own "Lord of Heaven," and that this is their true self.
* Conforming to Christ is a process with many steps, and a level of perfection is sought after by the low soul, the human soul, and the physical consciousness. The high soul and spirit of the individual, which stay in heaven, *are* at a high level of perfection. The deeper doctrine teaches that one's divine self, their Christ-Self, *is* their "Father."

"Be ye therefore perfect, even as your Father which is in heaven is perfect." (Matthew 5:48)

* During soul's incarnation on Earth, it gradually returns to its former consciousness level, and at translation, goes back to the level of heaven it is from. An exception would be if a particular soul had fallen, or started to fall, which is a possibility for any soul. It is rare, as when that begins to happen to a soul, help is dispatched, usually in the form of family or friends that incarnate at roughly the same time. Assisting that soul in trouble, and hopefully turning it around, will be a part of their mission. Souls routinely incarnate into groups of families and friends, that form a network of help if needed.
* As souls traverse the levels of heaven, they are constantly merging with the new level of themselves that they are attaining. The human soul merges with the low soul, which then strives to merge with the high soul; in turn, it will someday merge with its own spirit, and finally, when reaching the highest heaven, will become its divine self.

All of the outer sheaths will have then been shed, and one has become their very essence, a son/daughter of God, and a fully realized cell of Christ's body. One's very consciousness then *is* the Christ consciousness, the mind of Christ.

*   Quoting the sixth verse of the 82nd Psalm, Christ Jesus makes a point of telling the Jewish religious leaders that they are Gods. (John 10:34)

Gods have the ability to create, and this is true of soul; it has the ability to create, whether it be in creating forms out of the Word, or in creating its very self through its own imagination; soul becomes how it sees itself.

"For as he thinketh in his heart, so *is* he: …." (Proverbs 23:7)

*   The way creation works in the pure God heavens, (5th, 6th, 7th) is different than the way it happens in the lower four, dual heavens. In the positive God-heavens, creation is magical, like one might imagine; the Holy Word rushes to fill whatever soul wills and imagines instantaneously. Nothing in the God-planes exists but what soul, or a group of souls, is creating and sustaining at that very moment, including the entire heaven it is dwelling in.
*   In the lowest heavens, Christ created everything to be temporarily permanent, whether it be a form or state of consciousness. This means that through imagination and feeling, one creates by *attracting* created forms and states. It is a reflective opposite of true creation; in the God-heavens, one could create a car instantly; on Earth, one attracts one through buying it.
*   In the third and fourth heavens, souls can create forms out of those heavens' matter; however, while being extremely rapid, it is in successive steps, and the creation is temporal and of inferior quality.
*   Christ creates the lower dual worlds, maintains them for an age, and then destroys them. This is followed by a long rest for souls, equal in duration to the manifested creation, and then the cycle begins again; souls once again take on bodies, and the experiences that go with them; school resumes.

* Salvation breaks this cycle, as upon graduating to the fourth and fifth heaven, soul does not have to incarnate into the lower heavens again. They have finished inhabiting bodies that suffer birth and death in the lower heavens. Beginning in the *fifth heaven,* souls are deathless, and *completely* immortal in the kingdom of heaven.
* Souls graduating to the fifth heaven have also merged with the other half of themselves, (soul mate) and are now as they were before their journey into the lower heavens. Adam and Eve have become one. Neither half lose any individuality; to the contrary, it is increased. As soul evolves, it is constantly becoming a functioning part of some larger presence, whether it be in joining its other half, the body of consciousness in a new heaven, or eventually, Christ itself. One's arm does not lose its individuality because it is attached to a body.

"But they which shall be accounted worthy to obtain that world, and the resurrection from the dead, neither marry, nor are given in marriage: Neither can they die anymore: for they are equal unto the angels; and are the children of God, being the children of the resurrection." (Luke 20:35-36)

* Above (within) the seven heavens, there is an immense void with many levels that is without light or sound. There is a tremendous calm. The only light present is oneself. All is unmanifested. This is known as the heart of God, from which the Holy Word emanates. This region is home to the Archangels, Silent Watchers, and the ALMIGHTY ABSOLUTE GOD. Very little is known of this unimaginable region; even less is known of the ABSOLUTE.

"No man hath seen God at any time." (I John 4:12)

THE FIRST HEAVEN

The first heaven is usually called the Physical Plane, and the vibration of light here is so low that there is solid matter, and relative to higher heavens, it is very dark, even during the day. This plane has seven sub-levels, and each of them seven as well. In many systems of the heavens, the Physical Plane is considered a sub-level of the Astral Plane, the second heaven. The lower levels of this plane contain numerous hells and reform schools that are dark indeed. No soul stays in a hell forever but leaves once they have been purged, and the negative energy from their deeds has dissipated, allowing them to move on.

This plane includes all of the stars, galaxies and constellations that science knows of. Soul here is trapped by desires of the flesh and mind. The vast bulk of mankind is cut off from their own high soul, and their low soul is looking *out* into the world, identifying with the mind and its desires, instead of looking *within* to God. Jesus called them a "generation of vipers." (Matthew 23:33)

These worldly desires are often called the seven deadly sins: pride; greed; wrath; envy; lust; gluttony; and sloth. These sins are thought to be excessive abuses of one's natural faculties. In the Eastern teachings, they are called the five deadly passions, and are characterized as vanity, lust, anger, attachment, and ego (wrong identity). The Christian Bible is clear as glass on the "world" and its temptations.

"Love not the world, neither the things *that are* in the world. If any man love the world, the love of the Father is not in him. For all that *is* in the world, the lust of the flesh, and the lust of the eyes, and the pride of life, is not of the Father." (I John 2:15-16)

On the Physical Plane, life is coarse and very short, war is continuous, and change is endemic as the positive and negative forces are constantly engaged against each other. Cities are cesspools of overcrowded, crime-ridden hovels. Starvation and malnutrition are common. Hate and prejudice are everywhere. Evil has a panoply of avenues.

Many of the less evolved souls engage in crime, violence and evil; this too is part of their spiritual education, as shocking experiences, *with* their attending consequences, are needed to wake up and vivify their inner consciousness centers, which are in the beginning of their human incarnations, dormant potentialities.

This is eating from the tree of the knowledge of good and evil, but perhaps consuming the lowest hanging fruit; none the less, it is purposeful. Souls have seen it all; sometimes, the Lord has to use violent shocks to get a soul's attention.

The souls themselves are never killed or maimed, but they are trapped in their bodies, which may go through all manner of tortuous experiences. After an eternity, and much experience, souls get tired of the negative consequences that they are creating, and are ready to come to Christ, like a prodigal son/daughter that is tired of eating corn husks fed to the swine. (Luke 15:16)

More evolved souls, which have better control of their human vehicle, are beyond the need for violent, criminal events, but no one escapes the human chaos totally, as the nature of this heaven is to foster conflict, division, and change. This is purposeful, as it forces learning, growing, and individuality, which help prevent stagnation and staid conformity.

Most believers agree that they have learned the most under duress; they hated it, but they were forced to learn; one may see from this a purpose of the negative forces.

"For I am come to set a man at variance against his father, and the daughter against her mother, and the daughter in law against her mother in law." (Matthew 10:35)

"Think not that I am come to send peace on earth: I came not to send peace, but a sword." (Matthew 10:34)

In this present age, which is gradually nearing its end, sex is the most powerful force on Earth: most men are consumed by it, most women play to it, and the media is constantly portraying gratuitous sex and lust as though they are virtues. Sexual perversion and sexual diseases are rampant; pornography is mainstream.

Due to the fact Earth is nearing the end of a long cycle, the negative forces are much stronger than the positive forces. Man is bombarded with the carnal desires of the mind.

Even the religions are polluted; for example, millions of children have been sexually molested by gay pedophile priests in the Catholic church, eighty percent of them young boys; an untold number are yet to be uncovered in other denominations and religions, which reportedly may be worse.

"And [Jesus] said unto them, It is written, My house shall be called the house of prayer; but ye have made it a den of thieves." (Matthew 21:13)

"But as the days of Noe were, so shall also the coming of the Son of man be." (Matthew 24:37)

In the future, this downward spiral of negativity will lead to destruction of the entire heaven, and after a rather lengthy hiatus, it will be recreated and populated with souls once more. The Christ in Jesus called these souls "a generation of vipers," and refused to give them a sign, or speak of truth except in parable. (Matthew 3:7)

These "ages" begin very positively, very peacefully, and very spiritually, but over long periods of time, gradually degenerate into negativity and evil, before they come to an end and are destroyed. In the East, these ages are divided into the Golden Age, the Silver Age, the Bronze (Copper) Age, and the Iron Age; this current "generation" is presently in the Iron Age.

These ages are incredibly long: Christian Theosophy and Hinduism have given numbers for various cycles, that number in the trillions of years. One must realize that even the largest numbers mean nothing, as life is eternal: there was no beginning; there is no end.

"Heaven and earth shall pass away, but my words shall not pass away." (Matthew 24:35)

At the end of an age, souls are judged, and those found worthy, advance to the next age in their spiritual evolution. Those souls found wanting in their spiritual development are held back, and after a lengthy pause of rest and reintegration, become leaders and way showers for the next generation coming up.

It is very much like being held back a grade in school. This is a bit of unpleasantness for soul as they are near unconscious during these "rests." Souls are never forced to move ahead: free will is respected, and the amount of time taken to progress means nothing; there is *absolutely* no rush.

At this point in this generation's spiritual growth, there may be a correlation between passing the next judgement, and having had decided to go *with* God, instead of the "world."

"So shall it be at the end of the world: the angels shall come forth, and sever the wicked from among the just, And shall cast them into the furnace of fire: there shall be wailing and gnashing of teeth." (Matthew 13:49-50)

These cycles go on endlessly into eternity, as the lower four levels of heaven are periodically created, maintained, and destroyed. The three higher heavens are deathless and never destroyed; in addition, soul is never destroyed. Destroying a soul would mean destroying a part of Christ, which is impossible. All souls *eventually* make it back to God. Christ Jesus said that it was His Father's wish, that not one of His children should perish. (Matthew 18:14) God *does* get His will.

"And, Thou, Lord, in the beginning hast laid the foundation of the of the earth; and the heavens are the works of thine hands: They shall perish; but thou remainest; and they shall all wax old as doth a garment; And as a vesture shalt thou fold them up, and they shall be changed: but thou are the same, and thy years shall not fail." (Hebrews 1:10-12)

The first heaven, along with the other three lower heavens, has been called the illusion of reality. Things are not what they seem. One of the deepest illusions is that people are not who they think they are. They believe they are the mind, and if they believe in soul, believe it is their mind. Others believe that their emotional consciousness is the soul; many think they are their body, and that when their body dies, they also die. Total ignorance of man's innate divinity is ubiquitous.

Most are fascinated by the body's appearance, and spend large amounts of time and money on their face, figure, or dress. Others are consumed by what the body can do, whether in athletic contests or the arts. Looks are usually more important than character, and the public's heroes are either rich, famous, or exceptionally good looking. Many marry simply based on their partner's looks. Few realize that "true love" is love for God, and God's love for man.

Ironically, despite the importance given the body, few take care of their own, and obesity, disease, addiction, and gluttony are rampant. Cancers eat at the soul and body.

"(For many walk, of whom I have told you often, and now tell you even weeping, *that they are* the enemies of the cross of Christ: Whose end *is* destruction, whose God *is their* belly, and *whose* glory *is* in their shame, who mind earthly things.)" (Philippians 3:18-19)

A high percentage of the population is either using alcohol or drugs, whether legal or illegal. Millions are in therapy listening to worldly advice. Most individuals are terrified of death of the body; if they could, they would stay in this "hell" forever. The *illusion* of death is pervasive, and acts as a spiritual spur in all sorts of positive ways.

There are many other illusions as well: matter is simply slowed-down light; time, as experienced here, does not exist; eternity is now; and, what seems like space is full of the heavens within. An additional grievous illusion is that the things of the "world" can fulfill one; only Christ can fulfill one.

Despite putting a pretty face on things, nothing seems to escape corruption in the first heaven during this age and generation; even the religions, and the leaders running them, are often corrupt. Those feigning spirituality, are most often both in the world and of the world. The religions convince their adherents that they are saved by saying a few magic words, going to church, or being baptized; Christ is not a fool, nor is full salvation simply for the asking. An extremely high level of purity is needed to qualify for the kingdom of God.

"God that made the world and all things therein, seeing that he is Lord of heaven and earth, dwelleth not in temples made with human hands." (Acts 17:24)

In the first heaven, few read or know their own scriptures: sincerity is scarce, total commitment is rare, and for many, there is simply no time for daily devotions. Among the religious, the appearance of spirituality is the norm, and daily communion with Christ is seldom practiced. Most people are simply overwhelmed by daily challenges in attempting to survive in the world, and put little if any attention on God, until they are on their death bed. Suicides and drug overdoses are a main cause of death.

"Jesus said, I took my stand in the midst of the world, and in flesh I appeared to them.

I found them all drunk, and I did not find any of them thirsty. My soul ached for the children of humanity, because they are blind in their hearts and do not see, they came into the world empty, and they also seek to depart the world empty. But meanwhile they are drunk. When they shake off their wine, then they will change their ways." (Gospel of St. Thomas #28)

"Jesus said, Whoever has come to know the world has discovered a carcass, and whoever has discovered a carcass, to that person the world is not worthy." (Gospel of St. Thomas #56)

The deeper secrets know, that in spite of the spiritually gross conditions in the first heaven, especially towards the end of an age, this heaven, and all heavens, are stunningly perfect in every way, and *exactly* as Christ wants them to be; He is the author and creator of these conditions, and they are designed to teach souls the truth of God; they are first grade experiences, and the souls in the first heaven are mostly first graders.

Souls only experience what they have created; while it can appear as though they were thrown into the water to learn how to swim, the Divine Lifeguard is watching over them, and will not let them drown.

Justice and fairness are perfectly applied, with an overwhelming amount of mercy and compassion. Granted, *relative* to the higher heavens, the first heaven is dark and negative, and not unlike a reform school; none the less, it is perfectly designed and operated.

All negative criticisms of the first heaven, are made relative to higher heavens. Compared to even lower levels, Earth is a paradise, with wonderful things to enjoy, and endless beauty. There are also so many beautiful souls present.

Those thinking the world is out of control do not understand God's plan. The world does *not* need to be made a better place; the first grade does not need to be the second grade; souls need to graduate to the next grade. Those serving the world, are assisting those who maintain the world as it is, and paving the way for their own graduation to higher heavens.

The first heaven is extremely vast as modern telescopes have documented; its sub planes also have multiple levels, and are endless as well. Scientists state that the Milky Way has over 200 billion stars, and trillions of planets; all of these planets, and stars, have life at varying stages; in addition, the Milky Way is only one of quadrillions of galaxies, and this is only part of the first heaven, the smallest heaven. Christ's creation is incomprehensible, and millions of times vaster than any person could imagine.

As is true of all of the heavens, there is an immense difference between the lower end of a heaven, and the higher end. On this plane, there are primitive savages living alongside scientists and spiritual giants, with thousands of levels of growth between these two extremes.

One may be surviving on insects in a tropical jungle, or teaching in a Christian university.

Each level of heaven is a weaker carbon copy of the level above it; in addition, each heaven reflects the entire creation from top to bottom.

THE SECOND HEAVEN

"In my Father's house are many mansions: if it were not so, I would have told you." (John 14:2)

The second heaven is often called the Astral Plane, and not only is it immense in its entirety, but its seven sub planes, and the seven sub planes within each of them, are incredibly vast as well: it makes the first heaven look tiny.

It is at a higher vibration than the first heaven. Its lower sub planes are deep within the earth, while its highest reach the Moon's orbit. Souls do not see the sub planes above (within) them, or below them, so different are the vibration frequencies between these levels; what souls experience on each sub plane of a heaven is also vastly different.

There is no eating or drinking on the Astral Plane, and those souls addicted to drink, drugs, or food, suffer painful withdrawals that are even more intense than on Earth; they are so painful, that many will haunt places that serve such, and try to grasp at it vicariously, or obsess a victim so as to experience some relief.

There is not sleep or the need for it, and there is a continuous diffused brightness without darkness or a nighttime. An exception to this is the lowest sub plane, which is very dark indeed. Souls there are in their own created hell.

The astral body is much more ethereal than the physical body, and cannot be permanently disfigured or hurt, as it can reconstitute itself from astral matter, which is much more malleable than on the Physical Plane. Thought and imagination are much more powerful here, one can picture a tree in their garden and one will grow there.

Groups of souls collectively will imagine beautiful scenery, buildings, or other forms and create it. They collectively, through imagination, may even manifest famous people or prophets, all of which is illusionary. One's creative ability is very powerful here. This plane is four dimensional and one can see into things. Astral matter is much more porous and separated, and entities pass right through each other all the time.

This is also the home of the psychic sciences, from spiritualism to tarot card reading. Individuals and psychics channeling this plane's consciousness will have a degree of increased perception, but are unable to see anything clearly, including the future. The psychic arts are completely unreliable and dangerous, as they influence people and souls into all kinds of trouble. Most of the UFO activity on earth is also from this heaven, including geometric shapes like flying triangles, squares, or pyramids.

The lower sub planes of the second heaven are also the realm of ghosts and wandering spirits, most of whom have died an early unplanned death, due to suicide or violence; this prevents them from moving on, until their present lifetime's allotment of energy is consumed.

There are counterparts here of various paths and religions on Earth, mainly on the upper sub planes, which are beautiful and scenic. Their adherents have created what their imagination has been led to believe is heaven, with all manner of beautiful palaces and buildings. On the upper two sub planes, people are very beautiful, and very happy.

They do not work but spend their time on creative projects. Lifetimes can last many thousands of years.

Due to its strong karmic affinity for the physical body, a majority of the astral body is contained within the physical vehicle. The rest protruding from the body is called the aura. The astral body is full of swirling colors that very accurately reflect an individual's emotional states: negative emotions produce garish, muddy, and unattractive colors; noble and positive emotions produce beautiful pastels.

The study of the language of colors is a vast science, and there are many colors and shades of colors here unknown on the Physical Plane. There is an order of angels that flash uncountable shades of colors as their language.

An undeveloped person will have an astral body that is loosely organized, dense, dark, and not clearly outlined: it corresponds to the lowest of desires, whereas a developed person's astral form will be larger, clearly defined, and luminous, reflecting a more spiritual consciousness. A spiritually developed person's astral form appears as little sparkling stars, often with a train like a bridal dress, and their aura may be very large, extending far out from the body.

The astral body is a sheath for soul so that it might experience sensation, feeling, desire, and passion. It is often called the animal within man. Those on the lowest sub planes are totally ruled by base appetites and passions, whereas the higher one goes within the Astral Plane, the more positive and noble the emotions become.

The Christ within Jesus refers to the emotions as the heart, completely separate from mind and soul. The heart can be good or bad. Many mistakenly think their "heart," or their emotions are the soul, but while soul has feeling, it does not have any emotions. Christ in Jesus separates the two in the great commandment.

"Thou shalt love the Lord thy God with all thy heart, and with all thy soul, and with all thy mind." (Matthew 22:37)

"The heart *is* deceitful above all *things,* and desperately wicked: who can know it?" (Jeramiah 17:9)

Desires are an incentive to eating from the tree of the knowledge of good and evil. While negative desires can look problematic, it is not desire that is the problem, but what is desired. Immature souls will crave the worst in human nature; those souls who have mastered their emotions will love God and the things of the spirit.

One's emotions are the power behind one's love for things, be it sexual pleasure or God. It is the engine behind one's imagination, and without a strong emotional component, one's spiritual journey is weak and without power. The love for material things and romantic love, are precursors to spiritual love, which will blossom at a later stage of growth.

The emotional body is also a gateway to the mind, and if the emotions are not under control, the mind cannot think clearly. Emotional individuals see everything emotionally, and logical thinking is completely lost on them. One cannot argue with an emotional individual. It is self-evident that the emotions should be under one's control, and ideally, used in loving God and others.

Souls on the Astral Plane are attempting to expand their identity through marriage, families, groups, teams, cities, states, nations …. The search is on for who they are, and if it is a group that they can identify with, they feel larger and more important. How many times has one heard said, "family is everything," or noticed strong appeals for fealty towards a sex, team, religion, city, state, nation or belief. These identities are of the world; eventually, all will identify as soul.

When soul's physical body dies, it moves into the astral body, and it will have a shell around it comprised of desire energy, which is comprised of what that person desired in their last life. This shell will have layers which represent types of desire, corresponding to the sub planes of the Astral Heaven. To dissipate this energy, so that it can rise up through the levels of this plane, soul will progressively go through the lowest region of each sub plane; this is the hell and purgatory of the Catholic faith, and the *kama loka* of the Eastern religions. Soul spends as much time on the lowest end of each sub plane, as it takes to dissipate that type of desire energy in the shell surrounding it.

Those individuals consumed with base passions will spend much time on the lowest sub plane, which is a terrifying hell-like darkness, where souls feel as if they are being continually chased by the worst they can imagine. There are no real "hells" but in an individual's imagination; if that person is estranged from God, and is morally bankrupt, they experience the worst: one cannot compete with one's imagination on the Astral Plane. This is a place where heavy karma gets paid; souls come out of there determined to *not* repeat their mistakes.

On the next three sub planes above the seventh, souls are still concerned with persons and events on Earth from their last lifetime. On the sixth sub plane, it may be marriage, children, or friends that still draw one's presence and attention. On sub planes five and four it may be politics, religion, or the affairs of nations on Earth.

This preoccupation with Earth and one's last life time, fades as one rises through the sub planes. Soul is getting ready to enter the third heaven before reincarnation, or it may qualify to live in a higher heaven, and will continue to move upward.

Goodly souls that do not have base desires, or a strong attachment to worldly things, will skip "hell," and may go through "purgatory" in hours; those who have practiced evil, or those consumed with desires for worldly pleasure, may spend thousands of years on a particular sub plane, either in a hell, or some other sub level corresponding to that kind of desire. The idea is for soul to rise through these levels, dissipating these shells of desire energy that are imprisoning it, so that it may enter the third heaven.

If one is a sincere, deeply committed follower of Christ, one will meet their teacher or master on the Astral Plane within themselves, usually at night during sleep in a dream or vision. Christians will meet Christ Jesus, the Virgin Mary, or a favorite saint; Jews may see Moses, a Rabbi, or a notable Old Testament prophet; Hindus may meet with *Krishna, Shiva, or* their *guru*; Buddhists may possibly be taught by the *Buddha* or an esteemed monk; Sikhs may converse with *Guru Nanak*, or his successors; the American Indian may speak with *Manitou* or a famous chief: the secret teachings believe that in *all* instances, it would be Christ manifesting to that individual in a form that they could accept. Christ loves and protects those that love Him, and is not bothered by human names or titles: He will manifest to His children.

"He that hath my commandments, and keepeth them, he it is that loveth me: and he that loveth me shall be loved of my Father, and I will love him, and will manifest myself to him." (John 14:21)

"But in every nation he that feareth him, and worketh righteousness, is accepted with him." (Acts 10:35)

"Where there is neither Greek nor Jew, circumcision nor uncircumcision, Barbarian, Scythian, bond *nor* free: but Christ *is* all, and in all." (Colossians 3:11)

Souls committed to truth are also taught to hear the audible Word on this plane, and after the believer focuses on listening for it, usually in their devotions, they are able to begin enjoying its glorious sounds. Simply listening to the Word will propel the student into a deeper bond with Christ, and is considered a penultimate devotional activity.

It has been said: "To be calm is the greatest achievement." This could easily apply to all of soul's lower bodies, but it is especially true of the emotional body. When under Christ's control, it is peaceful; serene; calm; introspective; *still;* it is relaxed in Christ, and open to His guidance.

"And he arose, and rebuked the wind, and said unto the sea, Peace, be still. And the wind ceased, and there was a great calm." (Mark 4:39)

"He maketh me to lie down in green pastures: he leadeth me beside the still waters." (Psalm 23:2)

"Be still, and know that I *am* God: ...." (Psalm 46:10)

THE THIRD HEAVEN

The third heaven is divided into the Mental Plane, consisting of the four lowest sub planes of the third heaven, and the Causal Plane, consisting of the top three. One reason for this is that soul has a distinct body for each of these divisions. The Mental Plane is the plane of the lower mind functions and concrete thought.

Again, this heaven is so vast there is no way to quantify it. Its sub planes, which are also divided into seven sub levels, and they into seven again, are so vast that one could easily believe that any one of them could be the entire creation. As is usual, as one progresses in, there is a marked jump in the frequency of the vibrations, and the light is much brighter; this also applies as one moves up the sub planes of all heavens.

The power to create is much stronger in the third heaven; souls, through thought and imagination, have fashioned outrageous structures and landscapes of whatever they thought beautiful. Forms and structures are beginning to look less solid; one sees on this plane from a five-dimensional viewpoint. This does not change what one sees, but how they see it. Entities here are incredibly beautiful and very happy.

One of the very noticeable effects on arriving here is the absence of the astral body. One is free of the emotions and the intense desires that originate with that body, especially coarse and carnal desires; this gives a more spiritual feeling to this heaven.

Many religions and teachings have heavens here. These faiths practice the same beliefs as on Earth, and through group imagination, will even manifest the leader or savior of their religion, who will play the part as expected by the followers. This is illusory; however, the followers believe it to be true.

There are several attributes that soul wants to develop in its mental body: the ability to concentrate, remember, imagine, contemplate, meditate, and, to be able to stop all thought and be still, thereby being an open channel for guidance from within. For advanced students in Christ, a developed mental body can also be used to operate on the Mental Plane.

A good mind, properly directed, is a must for the sincere Christian, not only for properly studying, analyzing guidance, and applying it, but to receive that "still small voice" in the first place. The mind cannot *think* of guidance; it must *receive* it.

"Let this mind be in you, which was also in Christ Jesus." (Philippians 2:5)

"Study to shew thyself approved, a workman that needeth not to be ashamed, rightly dividing the word of truth." (II Timothy 2:15)

A good mind, not properly directed, is man's worst enemy.

"Because the carnal mind *is* enmity against God: for it is not subject to the law of God, neither indeed can be. So then they that are in the flesh cannot please God." (Romans 8:7-8)

The mind cannot think any more than a computer can think. It is totally dependent on its senses, programing, conditioning and learning. It can work out deductions, similar to what a computer can perform, but it is unable to inductively think.

For example, a mind may deduce from its senses that the Sun revolves around the Earth, (billions did) due to the fact it sees the Sun moving across the sky; whereas a mind receiving input from soul, induces that the Earth, being the inferior body, must be rotating as it travels around the Sun, thus creating the illusion that the Sun is orbiting the Earth. Inductive thinking is not dependent on the senses; it is dependent on soul.

The mind cannot operate outside its programming, come up with something new, or understand. All thinking and understanding comes from soul, and the great innovators, inventors, artists, and spiritual giants are in tune with soul, and are sensitized to its whisperings. A trained *still* mind can receive messages from soul, but does not initiate them. The Christ in Jesus mocked the mind.

"And which of you with taking thought can add to his stature one cubit?" (Luke 12:25) "Then answered Jesus and said unto them, verily, verily, I say unto you, The Son can do nothing of himself, but what he seeth the Father do: for whatever things so ever he doeth, these also doeth the Son likewise." (John 5:19)

As is true with the astral body, the mental body is a whirling collage of light streams and thought forms, that perfectly reflect the thoughts and attitudes of the individual. The mental body of those on the lowest sub planes is muddied and often filled with garish, putrid shades of color, due to selfish and evil thoughts; it is ill-defined and small.

As one rises through the sub levels, the hues of the mental sheath become more refined, with beautiful pastel lights, and ever so delicate shades of color; these reflect noble and unselfish thoughts. In addition, as one develops the mental body, it grows in size and becomes more luminous; its vibrations also increase in frequency. On both the Astral and Mental Planes, there is no hiding what one is feeling or thinking: one is an open book. Individuals on the Astral Plane believe that their emotions are the soul; on the Mental Plane, they believe their mental thoughts are the soul; both are in error.

There is a consciousness stream in the top of the third heaven that is a memory of the entire creation, called the *akashic* records. This includes everything since the beginning of this creation cycle, including one's own history of incarnations, and everything that took place within them. Souls here can access this stream of consciousness within themselves, and gain tremendous insight into their past, and the reasons for their situation in the present.

This is a tremendous development, as one is suddenly privy to the big picture, not only of their own existence, but everything else that has happened to the planet since its creation. This is a pivotal point in the life of soul, as it now aware of what it has to do to advance, and it begins to understand its own place in evolution. Soul is moving away from the world of sensation, (Astral Plane) into the world of ideas on the Mental Plane.

On the lowest mental sub planes, soul is still experiencing some of the effects of astral body desires, which are entwined with the mind. On the seventh sub plane, this might be a love of family and friends from their past life, although it is a more refined affection.

These desires fade and disappear on the higher sub levels. Unlike the Astral Plane, souls arriving at the Mental Plane awaken on the sub plane that most closely represents their mental thoughts and development: there is no automatic progression through all of the levels, and hell and purgatory are a thing of the past.

The sixth sub plane is characterized by religious devotion and worship, usually directed towards a divine being. They may engage in service for their particular path or religion, although their beliefs may be characterized as a rather blind faith, free of intellectual rigor. None the less, their devotion has positive results and is helpful in moving soul towards a more virtuous life.

On the fifth sub plane, one finds that devotion has the added element of work for a cause. Souls here are busily involved in grand schemes and projects that benefit mankind, whether it is religious or artistic. They want to help, and imagine themselves saving others, and helping their respective religion or art positively impact the masses. They are gradually turning away from worshipping deities, and directing their help towards the whole of mankind.

On the fourth sub plane, souls are becoming a purer channel for God, and are busy attempting to help the whole of mankind. Their thought processes are also becoming more abstract and less concrete, reading between the lines, and understanding what symbols and allegories mean. These souls are also becoming more interested in the esoteric or hidden teachings, and are moving away from a literal interpretation of scripture and art.

When a soul's body dies on Earth, and after it has passed through the levels of the Astral Plane, it progresses to the Mental Plane, and begins to mentally assimilate experiences from its last lifetime. Once they have been integrated, the mental body fades away, and one's essence moves into the causal body within. Unless soul is going further, it is now ready to reincarnate, and resume its experiences on the Physical Plane or Astral Plane in a new body.

Those souls that are more advanced will either continue moving up, or begin living in the top three sub planes of the third heaven, which are called the Causal Plane. The colors and lights of these regions are beyond description, and souls appear as lighted spheres of incredible beauty, with lovely shimmering hues radiating over the surface of their body; their level of awareness is on display for all to see.

The Causal Plane is a big step up for soul. In some respects, it is the home of the low soul, as it keeps its causal body through its many lifetimes, whereas its lower mental body, astral body, lunar body and physical body are new each lifetime. This is where the advanced human soul, who has raised their consciousness to this level, merges and unites with the low soul. The low soul will not shed its causal body until permanently moving into the fourth heaven.

On the third sub plane of the third heaven, which begins the Causal Plane, many souls are still semi-conscious, but either they are dreamily awaiting a new incarnation, or they are beginning to wake up. The more advanced begin to study their own past by accessing the akashic records, becoming aware of their own place in evolution, and what they have to do to move on. This is a pivotal point in soul's awareness that cannot be exaggerated. Dreaming, via lifetimes in the lower heavens, is becoming a thing of the past; soul is awaking, and becoming aware of its own divine inheritance.

"The Spirit itself beareth witness with our spirit, that we are the children of God: And if children, then heirs; heirs of God, and joint-heirs with Christ; if so be that we suffer with *him,* that we may be also glorified together." (Romans 8:16-17)

On the second sub plane of the third heaven, souls have become self-conscious, and are becoming more committed towards Christ; they have opened themselves to inner guidance from His Spirit, and are beginning to more consciously direct their personality towards the things of God. They are thinking more clearly; abstractions and profound ideas are now being understood. Instead of literally interpreting scripture, they are beginning to discern the metaphors and hidden meanings.

"But we speak the wisdom of God in a mystery, *even* the hidden *wisdom,* which God ordained before the world unto our glory: Which none of the princes of this world knew: for had they known *it,* they would not have crucified the Lord of glory." (I Corinthians 2:7-8)

"Jesus said, I will give you what no eye has seen, and what no ear has heard, and what no hand has touched, and what has never occurred to the human mind." (St. Thomas Gospel #17)

Believers in this heaven are also continuing work on integrating their feminine and masculine consciousness. The feminine consciousness in man, called the anima, must be understood and incorporated into one's overall consciousness; likewise, the masculine consciousness in women, called the animus, must be unshackled and utilized.

Soul, which is above both of these, wants the ability to use either or both in its channeling. Often times, believers who are being successful in integrating their less dominant side, will have dreams of marriage.

On the first sub plane of the Causal Plane, which is also the top of the third heaven, souls have become self-directed and are becoming ready for advancement to the fourth heaven. These souls have committed themselves to helping the divine cause, and many teachings believe that their leaders and masters are living here, including well-known teachers from Christian Theosophy and other Christian disciplines, both esoteric and exoteric. These "leaders" are good teachers, but they themselves have not yet entered the kingdom of heaven, which begins in the fifth heaven.

These souls are realizing that they are not the personality, an illusion that has bedeviled them for eons. There are mental giants and geniuses here, inspired artists and philosophers, and souls living here have fallen into a deep love of God.

Ever since the individual accepted Christ into their life, teachers, disciples and adepts have been teaching and helping them learn, mostly at night during sleep; this includes taking them on visits to higher planes inside themselves, and also outside themselves. They will gradually be made aware of this in their physical consciousness, although conscious experiences are rare: they are given by Christ and cannot be had for the asking, nor is there any workable method to obtain them at will.

In addition, soul is beginning to enjoy a deeper relationship with the Holy Spirit, and believers may notice that the Holy Spirit is beginning to communicate with them, by increasing the audible life stream's volume at particularly significant moments. The timing of these occurrences is exact, and semi-rare.

THE FOURTH HEAVEN

The fourth heaven has several names depending on one's orientation. In the East, it is often called *Par Brahm* or the Bliss Plane. In the West, it is often called the high Mental Plane, the Buddhic Plane, or the Wisdom Plane. The very top of this heaven contains the unconscious. The fourth heaven, although dual, and ruled by the mind, is very close to soul.

Souls dwelling on the subjective side of the fourth heaven have progressed beyond the need for reincarnating into the lower heavens. They are indescribably joyful, and the body used here is often called the bliss sheath. It is the last of the dual heavens and souls here are very advanced compared to the levels below. The objective side of this heaven contains advanced civilizations, technology, and solar alliances that make *Star Wars* look like kiddie land.

This heaven produces a tremendous realization of unity, as the dual forces are getting very close to the point at which they merge. All feelings of separateness seem to fade, and soul further realizes its oneness with all souls, whether they be higher than itself or lower. This feeling of identification and brotherhood with others is so intense, that many feel they have lost all individuality, and are simply a part of the whole.

This is understandable but incorrect; soul always retains its individuality, no matter what level or group it merges with. Every atom in Christ's body is an individual while being a part of one gigantic whole. Often times, this heaven is called the home of cosmic consciousness; souls here feel that they are one with everything, and can identify with everyone. Many mystics and saints working from this heaven have reported incredible visions of the Light, manifesting to them in life-changing experiences.

This heaven is so vast that it is beyond objective description; the souls' bodies here are so bright that one could not look in their direction with human eyes lest instant blindness occur. Although it contains seven sub planes, it is often divided into three regions. Each of these regions deal with separate stages of soul's growth.

In general, the first region deals with a thorough purification of the higher mind, the second region involves identifying one's true self, (soul) and the third region, corresponding to the unconscious, involves becoming soul.

In the East, gaining this heaven means receiving the first initiation, when the consciousness has moved from the causal body into the high mental body; they term this self-realization, when one begins *realizing* that they are soul. In the West, Christians call this salvation. In both systems, soul completes this birth of spirit in the fifth heaven.

This event is accompanied by a game-changing event, perhaps the greatest event in soul's existence since accepting Christ. The individual glimpses their own radiant self, usually when it is moving out of the causal body, into the high mental body. It is ablaze with a radiant splendor, and viewing it is a tremendous shock. This is the first *possible* viewing of one's very own shining self.

This is called the *Augoeides* in the West, the viewing of the luminous self. This event is the beginning of several possible viewings of one's own self, during further advances in Christ. For unknown reasons, not all souls register this viewing, or somehow do not field it, and have to wait until further advances in this heaven, before being allowed to view their own inner radiance. Perhaps the glimpsing of their luminous body was too fast to properly register, or the recipient thought it something imaginative.

This is a *very* exalted event, and rare in this present "generation" on Earth.

"Enter ye at the strait [narrow] gate: for wide *is* the gate, and broad *is* the way, that leadeth to destruction, and many there be which go in thereat: Because strait *is* the gate, and narrow *is* the way, which leadeth unto life, and few there be that find it." (Matthew 7:13-14)

This event is so grandiose and impactful, that it can take years to understand exactly what has happened. The human soul and the human consciousness, which have glimpsed this vision, become unbalanced, and are lost as to how to interpret this viewing correctly.

The individual usually assumes that they must be a special entity, so overwhelming is their own radiant appearance. They often believe they must be a saint, prophet, or some famous savior, even Jesus Himself. They do not realize that this happens to every soul arriving here; they are not special in the way they may be thinking. This event is the beginning revelation of the mystery of the ages, and the hidden wisdom: one is a part of Christ. Further viewings will reveal the same truth.

"Where there is neither Greek nor Jew, circumcision nor uncircumcision, Barbarian, Scythian, bond *nor* free: but Christ *is* all, and in all." (Colossians 3:11)

"But we speak the wisdom of God in a mystery, *even* the hidden *wisdom*, which God ordained before the world unto our glory: Which none of the princes of this world knew: for had they known *it*, they would not have crucified the Lord of glory…. But God hath revealed *them* unto us by his Spirit: for the Spirit searcheth all things, yea, the deep things of God." (I Corinthians 2:7-8,10)

When soul enters the fourth heaven, it has been stripped of its material bodies below, and it undergoes a deep purification and purging of its mind. After being cleansed, it is now freer of the lower minds' influence, and their accompanying baggage.

Spiritual discernment is increased as one begins to reason intuitively, and more accurately discern the high soul's voice. It still may be without clarification as to what it witnessed in moving into this sheath, but soul is now ready for an event that will further clarify and transform its very existence.

This occurs when soul enters a region located in the middle of the fourth heaven. It is the vision of the high soul, in its fifth heaven's body. Not only does the low soul view this glorious manifestation, but it also views what the high soul is engaged in doing in this heaven, and the enormous amount of souls being helped.

This will completely upend an individual's old life, and everything in their world will undergo a massive transformation. This is doubly true for those who missed the first glimpsing of their higher self. Seeing is believing, and these individuals have seen the truth with their own eyes. This is witnessed all the way down to the physical consciousness, and is the second (first?) viewing of one's own radiant self. This event *is* a given.

"Therefore if any man *be* in Christ, *he is* a new creature: old things are passed away; behold, all things are become new." (II Corinthians 5:17)

The secret teachings believe that this is the beginning of salvation; the completion of salvation will occur when the low soul moves into the fifth heaven, and merges with the deeper part of itself it viewed.

"For our conversation is in heaven; from whence also we look for the Saviour, the Lord Jesus Christ: Who shall change our vile body, that it may be fashioned like unto his glorious body, according to the working whereby he is able even to subdue all things unto himself." (Philippians 3:20-21)

The low soul, the human soul, and the human consciousness, have looked into a celestial mirror and seen who their master really is. Usually, if not always, this event is so gigantic, and the vision of its radiant soul body so incredibly amazing, that the individual experiencing this continues believing, or begins believing, that they must be a special person.

The individual experiencing this will usually be quite unbalanced for a time, and need much spiritual contemplation to rebalance themselves in this new state of consciousness; there is no going back to the way it was; one cannot "unsee" what they viewed, nor will they ever forget it. This is a life-altering experience.

The low soul recognizes that it *is* the high soul which it has viewed, but does not *realize* it as of yet; the low soul has not *identified as* it, and does not have the high soul's consciousness. This usually leads to the low soul misinterpreting what happened, and subsequently, it becomes enamored of itself.

Consequently, they often wish to be recognized as a great soul, someone that deserves special recognition and deifying, and it is this desire which will keep them imprisoned in the fourth heaven until they can pierce through this illusion, and move into the fifth heaven. This is a self-inflicted chimera originating within its own unconscious body.

They continue to identify as the low soul, which is still in its mental body, and beheld this celestial vision, instead of identifying *as* the part of themselves they viewed, the high soul in its soul body. The low soul often believes it has finished the journey and entered the seventh heaven. It would be similar to a student in elementary school thinking that they had graduated from the university with a Ph.D.

The challenge of identifying as the high soul is expressed in the East as follows: "*that I am*" ("*tat tvam asi*"). This is (figuratively) uttered by the low soul upon viewing the high soul in its soul body. *Identifying* as one's higher soul, merging and blending with it through direct experience, is the next step. This will include adopting a fifth heaven's point of view, and living it; this is the first level of the Christ consciousness, and the mind of Christ.

Those stalled in the fourth heaven are still operating out of the mind, and the mind likes to believe that it is not only the low soul, but that it is also the high soul; it is neither. The mind will convince the individual that they are already realized and in the higher God planes.

In addition, they will believe that their methodology and personal will have played an instrumental role in obtaining their imagined station. They are anxious to tell others what they must do to be realized, and just how to do it, whereas the truth of the matter is that they themselves are not yet realized. Before realization, all of what is left of their personal will and ego, will have to be given up to Christ.

"Trust the Lord with all thy heart; and lean not unto thine own understanding." (Proverbs 3:5)

"Be not wise in thine own eyes…." (Proverbs 3:7)

In a sense, there is no *way* or *method* to *get* salvation. It is *given* by Christ's *grace*, when one has surrendered everything to God, and implemented their guidance to conform to Christ. No one is ever worthy, or qualifies to earn it, but those that are given salvation, have learned to *let* Christ have His way with them.

"For by grace are ye saved through faith; and that not of yourselves: it is the gift of God. Not of works, lest any man should boast." (Ephesians 2:8-9)

"In whom also we have obtained an inheritance, being predestinated according to the purpose of him who worketh all things after the counsel of his own will: That we should be to the praise who first trusted in Christ." (Ephesians 1:11-12)

The illusions ensnaring souls in the fourth heaven are of herculean strength, and many souls languish in this heaven for eons, often times until the end of the cycle when this level is destroyed. One of the reasons these illusions are so powerful, is that the souls here, besides fielding an extremely high consciousness, can create anything they wish in a heartbeat; however, it is still out of the fourth heaven's energies and matter, often called the universal mind power, and is temporal and inferior.

A further difference is that reflective creation in the fourth heaven occurs in sequential steps, albeit incredibly fast, unlike creation out of spirit in the positive heavens, which is instantaneous. These differences escape the notice of souls in the fourth heaven, and they usually believe that they have entered the kingdom of God.

The problem here is that the individual has not fully self-surrendered to Christ. They are still operating from a mental consciousness that is not pure. Their high soul's guidance has been filtered by their unconscious mind sheath, located at the top of this heaven: this sheath still has age old desires, especially for praise, recognition, and titles; these desires block not only the truth, but the high soul's guidance as well. One does not fall on their knees to Christ; one falls flat on their face...with arms to the side.

Members of the Pharisee's, Scribes and the Sanhedrin in Jesus' time were probably from this heaven. They were trained thinkers, incredibly educated, who felt they knew everything; Jesus pointed out that they knew absolutely nothing, and were totally corrupt. The same souls are here again, and still as ignorant as before.

It is known that souls here can be told nothing, so confident and enamored are they of their imagined status. It is difficult to listen to what one must do to advance, when one thinks that it has already been accomplished. It will take a very painful self-analysis to ferret these desires out, an analysis that must be based on guidance from the Holy Spirit and the high soul. There are two developments that make solving this very difficult illusion possible.

The first development is referred to as the dark night of the soul, an epithet coined by the mystic, St. John of the Cross, in his famous 16th century poem, *The Dark Night of the Soul*. This is also known as the crucifixion of the ego, picking up one's cross, or being crucified with Christ; one's life is completely flattened. Everything seems to collapse, and nothing seems to go right. Often times, one is reduced to a penniless state, and is deserted by family and friends. One feels God has forsaken them. It feels worse than death.

The believer is faced with the recognition that they are totally powerless, totally ignorant, totally insignificant, totally alone, and totally dependent on Christ. This "dark night" may last for years or even lifetimes; it may occur either before one's celestial vision of the high soul, or more often, after. It is the ultimate takedown and one is left totally gutted. Soul must learn to create their way out of this death, see through its unconscious desires, and give them up to Christ; a deep selflessness is required.

A second ongoing development that helps soul see the correct direction, is an increased relationship with the audible Holy Spirit. Since their journey through the third heaven, those in pursuit of discipleship have had the opportunity of listening to this marvelous river of sound with their inner ears, and have experienced hearing the Holy Spirit increase the volume of its music at perfectly timed moments. Those that experience this phenomenon have grown increasingly adept at interpreting the Holy Spirit's messages. These wonderful occurrences are infrequent and usually unforgettable.

"Amazing grace, how sweet the sound, that saved a wretch like me." (Amazing Grace hymn)

These communications are deciphered intuitively, and through experience, one becomes proficient in understanding what is being messaged, having had been able to check their interpretations in retrospect. Usually, one just knows, and somehow the communication has been laid on one's heart. These whisperings from Christ, relayed through one's own spirit and soul, are so precious, so incredibly life-saving, that they are difficult to adequately qualify. Just *one* of these experiences can completely change one's life.

The secret teachings believe that this relationship with the audible Holy Spirit is necessary to advance into the fifth heaven. One needs both the Light and the Sound to enter the kingdom of God.

In addition, at this point, those deep in Christ are not only regularly visiting the heavens within themselves, disciples and high teachers are instructing soul on how to leave the physical vehicle, and venture into the universes outside of the body.

The physical consciousness never controls the process of soul leaving the body, but can facilitate it through stillness and imagination; it can also soul travel in a reflective way by raising its state of consciousness. For example, if one were depressed, and through prayer and devotions raised their consciousness, thereby vanquishing the negative feelings, they would be travelling to higher heavens in a very real way. The higher heavens *are* high states of conscious.

THE FIFTH HEAVEN

The fifth heaven is a neutral heaven, much like any center space between two opposing magnetic fields. There is not a crystal-clear demarcation between the top of the fourth heaven and the fifth, and there is similarly not a clear line of separation between the top of the fifth heaven and the sixth. Instead, in both cases there is a gradual transition. Form is seriously faded on this level; there is increased light and a tremendous jump in perception. Soul knows everything about whatever it puts its attention on.

The low soul has moved out of the unconscious sheath at the top of the fourth heaven into the soul body, and it is now free of all of its dual worlds' sheaths. The low soul's body at this level is immense; it is so bright that it is compared to several large suns. The low soul at this level is fully free, and is now above the dual worlds that are periodically destroyed and recreated. Soul has awakened from its dream in the lower heavens. This is the heaven where soul previously became fully personified in its descent from above.

Souls at this level are considered adepts, masters, disciple/teachers, or high saints. Many of these souls are on missions that help channel the Holy Spirit into the heavens below. Others are on various missions to help souls in the dual worlds. These adepts have reentered the Garden of Eden, and have eaten from the tree of life. They are fully immortal.

"He that hath an ear, let him hear what the Spirit saith unto the churches; To him that overcometh will I give to eat of the tree of life, which is in the midst of the paradise of God." (Revelation 2:7)

These souls have also learned to leave the physical body at their own volition without assistance, and will begin working on how to stay out of the body permanently. Soul is anxious to perfect this, to avoid being trapped in the body during mental or emotional disturbances by the physical consciousness. Once they master this, they will run their body from a higher dimension. The human consciousness will experience this ability by soul to vacate the human vehicle, but cannot itself initiate it.

The goal in the fifth heaven is to complete salvation by fully *identifying* as soul in its soul body, merging with its consciousness, and establishing itself in this heaven. There are many souls that are taken to this region as aspirants to learn and study, usually by masters and teachers in Christ that are living at this level, but establishing one's home here is the goal.

There is a huge difference between visiting here for learning purposes, versus being able to live here. Reaching this level of heaven is uncommon with the present generation on earth; however, eventually, every one of them will accomplish it.

"Jesus said, I shall choose you, one out of a thousand, and two out of ten thousand, and they shall stand as a single one." (Gospel of St. Thomas #23)

"Enter ye in at the strait [narrow] gate: for wide *is* the gate, and broad *is* the way, that leadeth to destruction, and many there be which go in thereat: Because strait *is* the gate, and narrow *is* the way, which leadeth unto life, and few there be that find it." (Matthew 7:13-14)

The fifth heaven is considered the first level of the Christ consciousness; this profound consciousness is a deep level of perception and knowingness, that originates from the very inner most part of one's being. It is similar to looking through Christ's eyes. At this level, soul cannot tell the difference between itself and the Holy Spirit. It has gained the consciousness associated with the mind of Christ. This consciousness is impossible to accurately describe; it is all-knowing, yet the opposite of thinking. It can seem irrational and wild, but is not.

"Let this mind be in you, that was also in Christ Jesus." (Philippians 2:5)

This profound consciousness is received by the physical consciousness through a total absence of thought. This practice of not thinking, similar to a state of semi-trance, is called *meditation, stillness, musing,* or *pondering* in the Holy Bible. Thinking blocks the Christ consciousness; meditation, stillness, or contemplation, create the conditions to receive it. The mind cannot *think* of guidance; it is a machine and *must* field it when still; this is absolute. One acts by initiating the conditions to be action less and receive it.

"When I remember thee upon my bed, *and* meditate on thee in the *night* watches." (Psalm 63:6)

"Till I come, give attendance to reading, to exhortation, to doctrine. Meditate upon these things; give thyself wholly to them; that thy profiting may appear to all." (I Timothy 4:13,15)

"But his delight *is* in the law of the Lord; and in his law doth he meditate day and night." (Psalm 1:2)

"Be still, and know that I *am* God…." (Psalms 46:10)

"…Peace, be still." (Mark 4:39)

"…he leadeth me beside the still waters." (Psalm 23:2)

"…a still small voice." (I Kings 19:12)

"Ponder the path of thy feet, and let all thy ways be established." (Proverbs 4:26)

"Every way of man *is* right in his own eyes: but the LORD pondereth the hearts." (Proverbs 21:2)

In receiving this deep, magical consciousness, an unintended phenomenon begins: while one can see into others like an open book, one can also see into themselves as well like never before, and suddenly, one realizes that they are not pure at all. Deep layers of ego and pride are revealed; hidden character flaws are suddenly apparent, like boils on the skin's surface, and a whole new level of purification is suddenly needed. One was blind, now they can see; this will lead to a complete transformation of one's life from A to Z.

One of the attendant miracles soul receives when establishing themselves in the fifth heaven, is that they have become one with the Holy Spirit; and, since the Holy Spirit is existent everywhere, soul can be everywhere; soul has become omnipresent, and if desired, can expand its spirit to completely include the entire creation.

This heaven also brings soul a tremendous feeling of freedom that seems to touch everything; freedom *is* happiness, and two of the greatest freedoms soul experiences here, are freedom from death, and freedom from their own ego and mind.

Souls established here also have powers over the heavens below, and can manipulate the lower world's forces at will. This is very seldom done, as changing what the spiritual energies are doing in the lower heavens, carries a high risk of unintended consequences, consequences they would be responsible for. Instead, souls here use their powers to change and perfect themselves, becoming a purer channel for Christ. As to the lower heavens, "it's best to let the Sun shine as it will." (Sohang)

After soul has made good progress in establishing itself in the fifth heaven, it is ready for a third possible viewing of itself. This momentous event involves the low soul viewing the high soul without any protective sheath. This awesome occurrence is beyond words, as the high soul appears Christ-like with one's own visage, and through images, foretells what is ahead for the individual. This vision transcends grandiloquent descriptions.

"Beloved, now we are the sons of God, and it doth not yet appear what we shall be: but we know that, when he shall appear, we shall be like him; for we shall see him as he is." (I John 3:2)

"And in the midst of the seven candlesticks *one* like unto the Son of man, clothed with a garment down to the foot and girt about the paps with a golden girdle. His head and *his* hairs *were* white like wool, as white as snow; and his eyes *were* as a flame of fire; And his feet like unto fine brass, as if they burned in a furnace; and his voice as the sound of many waters. And he had in his right hand seven stars: and out of his mouth went a sharp twoedged sword: and his countenance *was* as the sun shineth in his strength." (Revelation 1:13-16)

These encounters with the luminous self are difficult to parse and categorize; multiple parts of oneself are simultaneously taking part, and these visions happen in many different ways along the lines of the individual's own personality. One is watching parts of oneself watching other parts of oneself watching…. These viewings of the luminous selves have been written about throughout the centuries by saints, religious figures and philosophers. Jesus let three of His disciples see His Luminous Self before their very eyes.

"And after six days Jesus taketh Peter, James, and John his brother, and bringeth them up into an high mountain apart, And was transfigured before them: and his face did shine as the sun, and his raiment was white as the light." (Matthew 17:1)

The Persian *Sufis* refer to the vision of the *Resplendent One;* the Greeks describe viewing the *Self-Shining One* in the pure light, the *Augoeides;* the Christian Theosophists write of the *Radiance,* Hindus have referred to it as the *Radiant Self,* and many Christians call it one's *Guardian Angel,* or the *Higher Self.* These potential experiences can occur in many different ways and defy clear definition, subjectively, or objectively; however, they will happen at particular points in soul's growth.

"He that hath my commandments, and keepeth them, he it is that loveth me: and he that loveth me shall be loved of my father, and I will love him, and will manifest myself to him." (John 14:21)

"…I the Lord will make myself known to him in a vision, *and* will speak unto him in a dream." (Numbers 12:6)

An additional vision that the human consciousness often experiences in the fifth heaven, is that of the Cosmic Man, which appears to be perhaps a million miles in height. This is a symbolic viewing of the incredible channel that runs this heaven, and soul's relationship to it. One is also granted knowledge of souls' ultimate goal. Soul has become a realized cell of the body of Christ, and is no longer a prisoner of the lower world's bodies and sheaths: soul is free.

This freedom is beyond definition, as is the Christ Consciousness that goes with it.

"Now ye are the body of Christ, and members in particular." (I Corinthians 12:27)

THE SIXTH HEAVEN

The sixth heaven is the first heaven that is totally positive, and the peace and ecstasy experienced by soul, which has shed the last of its bodies, is indescribable; the low soul has merged with the high soul and they have become one. Soul has shed much of its individuality and is no longer fully personified; it is transitioning into *being* pure spirit.

"Then shall the dust return to the earth as it was: and the spirit shall return unto God who gave it." (Ecclesiastics 12:7)

A reason for the increased sublimity in this heaven, is that there is no longer a downward pull of desire for experience and manifestation in the lower heavens. This purposeful force, called *trishna* in the Eastern religions, is what originally attracted the unrealized soul into the lower heavens for experience, (Eve's apple) and being above it is like a weight off soul's shoulders. The spiritual forces acting on soul are now pulling it ever upward, and as one rises upward, this force becomes increasingly stronger.

This heaven is totally pure, ablaze with light, and so large that it is called endless. Some systems of thought divide this heaven into several heavens so large is it. Since there is not any space, separation between levels is caused by differing levels of consciousness.

There is a crystal-clear clarity and cleanliness about everything that is immediately noted: it is though one took off sunglasses that they were unaware of wearing. For perhaps the first time, there is a total absence of any kind of dust, dirt, or extraneous particles; this purity of the atmosphere, and everything else, shocks one visually; it is way beyond clean.

Although form is fading, and there does not seem to be any solid ground, there is a beauty present that is so lovely and peaceful, that it feels as though soul is vacationing in some south sea paradise. There is a relaxation here that is greater than restful. These positive God worlds are heavens of pure knowingness; soul instantly knows whatever it puts its attention on, and it can place attention in many different directions simultaneously. If necessary, it can run multiple low souls in multiple dimensions simultaneously; this can involve huge numbers.

Souls here are so anxious to serve that they will jump at any opportunity to help: not because they have to, not because they have been assigned to, but because they so badly *desire* to. It is an overwhelming desire to help in any way they can, and souls here are either waiting to serve, or have devised gigantic missions to help in this heaven, or the worlds below. Souls here have more fully realized Christ's incredible love.

Every soul here is busy with something, while enjoying the most satisfying peace. Souls here are not assigned a mission but choose how and where they wish to serve; it usually involves a mission where soul feels it can make a difference.

This results in souls often choosing missions that are impossible to fulfill. There is a relative naiveté among souls on this level, as they have not fully realized the slow and snail-like pace of eternity. Furthermore, they may not have fully understood that everything is already perfectly in place; there are not any emergencies anywhere. Most missions involve *keeping* things in place.

In addition, further advancements are agonizingly slow, and the spiritual lessons are thorough. There is an aphorism in the East that addresses this facet of eternity; it is considered absolute truth: "The mill of God grinds slowly, and exceedingly fine." Soul's vibration rate and consciousness *must* match the heaven it wishes to live in; realizations, and their application, take extensive experience; much experience takes much time.

This is one of the reasons why heaven cannot be given one; nor can a savior take soul to a high heaven to live. Soul must have a level of consciousness and awareness that matches those high heavens it would like to reside in. Christ teaches, protects, and helps souls learn what they have to, so that they may advance to these paradises.

One of the more common missions in the sixth heaven, is channeling the Word to the worlds below. This is more involved than one might expect, and souls study and work on how and what they are channeling. It is somewhat like musical composing, and if one were to see one of these souls channeling the Holy Spirit, they would be awed at the sight, not only at the size of these channels, but the gigantic streams of spirit that are pouring through them to the worlds below. No one would believe a description of them: no one. Many of these channels are larger than this solar system.

"For we are laborers together with God: ye are God's husbandry, *ye are* God's building." (I Corinthians 3:9)

There are many categories of souls here in the sixth heaven: some are recent arrivals from the worlds below and are on their way up; others have been here for untold ages, and are somewhat permanent residents of this heaven; there are also souls getting ready for the worlds below that have never ventured out from this Garden of Eden. There are orders of angels here, and souls from all over creation that are difficult to classify. Souls here are complete, in that they have joined their masculine and feminine halves, or have not separated them yet for the Lord's school below.

"But they which shall be accounted worthy to obtain that world, and the resurrection from the dead, neither marry, nor are given in marriage: Neither can they die anymore: for they are equal to the angels; and are the children of God, being the children of the resurrection." (Luke 20:35-36)

It is worth noting that it is possible for souls here to fall back into the lower worlds; in addition, sometimes a soul may revisit a lower heaven to refresh its commitment and consciousness. As said, soul's vibration rate must match the heaven it is living in or it will find itself in a lower heaven. Anything negative or impure cannot exist in the kingdom of God; this is one reason instant salvation is impossible.

Souls that have advanced to this heaven are realizing that they are not only perfectly aligned with spirit, they *are* pure spirit. This results in a shifting of individuality, from the personal to the whole, and soul/spirit is no longer fully personified or individualized; none the less, one as spirit still *is* an individual; every advancement by soul *increases* the individuality.

Soul/spirit in this heaven helps carry out the Holy Spirit's agenda, and this results in incredible missions on Christ's behalf, which does it all through one's very being. The heavens are not sustained by magic; they are managed and run by Christ through His channels; it *is* a *perfect* government.

The physical consciousness will experience a taste of what soul is doing in visions; one individual can change the whole creation if acting as a high-level channel for Christ; of course, they must have the capacity and evolvement to handle gigantic channeling. Jesus the Christ is a most wonderful example of this. As Christ, Jesus impacted the entire seven heavens, not just Earth.

"But when they deliver you up, take no thought how or what ye shall speak: for it shall be given you in that same hour what ye shall speak. For it is not you that speak, but the Spirit of your Father which speaketh in you." (Matthew 10:19-20)

THE SEVENTH HEAVEN

The seventh heaven is often divided into two sections, although like the other heavens, there is an increase in light and sound as one journeys inward through this heaven; its intensity here is unspeakable. This is where manifest creation begins, and it is also where it ends. There is no way to encompass the tiniest fraction of this. Galaxies by the zillions are a speck of nothing in this tornado of light and sound.

The beginning of this heaven concerns the imparting of divine wisdom, and so elevated and profound is this consciousness, that everything below this level is simply considered divine information and knowledge. This region is approaching the highest level of the Christ Consciousness.

"Happy *is* the man *that* findeth wisdom, and the man *that* getteth understanding.... She *is* more precious than rubies: and all the things thou canst desire are not to be compared unto her." (Proverbs 3:13,15)

"Jesus said: he who will drink from my mouth will become like me. I myself shall become he, and the things that are hidden will be revealed to him." (Gospel of St. Thomas #108)

The high soul has merged into its own spirit; it is no longer personified or individualized, even though it is more of an individual now than ever before.

Formerly, as spirit, it placed a *part* of itself in the sixth heaven as a high soul; and, when a *piece* of that consciousness descended into a soul body in the fifth heaven, it became fully personified and individualized.

"And the very God of peace sanctify you wholly; and I *pray God* your whole spirit and soul and body be preserved blameless unto the coming of our Lord Jesus Christ." (I Thessalonians 5:23)

It appears to be raining and snowing light in the beginning of this heaven; it has wildly increased in intensity, and is like some incredibly heavy blizzard. The sounds have increased tremendously, and are much greater than the light. At the lower end of this heaven is a vast ocean of unrealized souls, created by continuous reactions off the body of the Lord's channel who administers this heaven. IT is nameless.

When one meets their self at this level within oneself, it is preceded by a tremendous, thunderous sound, as though this spirt has violently ripped opened dimensions to appear. Its form is usually a ball of light, vibrating, humming and crackling with an insane power; the sound is much greater than the light in this heaven. This is the fourth possible viewing of oneself, and like the first three, it is experienced by the physical consciousness as well in a vision; all visions are given by Christ's grace.

This viewing is incredibly dramatic; one is left totally shaken to the core. The spirit inhabiting this level of oneself, which is a microcosm of the same spirit governing this entire heaven, is known as the custodian of Christ's power, and it is completely different than one might expect.

This part of oneself seems cold, distant, infinitely powerful, seemingly violent, and apparently contemptuous of man; there is not any communication with this channel of Christ; its actions appear disdainful, and one feels like a straw in the middle of a hurricane.

One is attacked with a force that cannot be resisted, and feels as though they have been grabbed by a large steam shovel, without being able to do a thing about it; the believer is along for the ride, and discovers that they are no more than a puppet completely controlled by Christ. One completely resigns themselves to this power; at this point, one *desires so very much* to be controlled by Christ's power.

"…but the thunder of his power who can understand?" (Job: 26:14)

There is an attendant wonderfulness with this experience that leaves one supercharged with excitement, awe and bliss; soul/spirit *wants* to be a puppet and servant of Christ!

"For he that is called in the Lord, *being* a servant, is the Lord's freeman: likewise also he that is called, *being* free, is Christ's servant." (I Corinthians 7:22)

One of the major areas focused on in the beginning of Spirit's experience here, is the realization of eternity. This realization concerns the scope and sequence of *real time* in creation. Everything concerning duration is expanded exponentially, and one finds that the pace of soul's growth, and everything else, is many times slower than previously thought. Eternity stretches out into infinity without end, and the time soul thought was needed to accomplish a particular level of growth, is extended beyond belief: way beyond belief. This is something that cannot be grasped by the human mind.

This expansion of time, and the unmeasurable vastness of Christ's creation, are so immense, that many spirits arriving here for the first time, become spiritually ill, and retreat to a level below for more experience. There is not a way to quicken eternity. Time means nothing; eternity is now, and it always will be. There is no past or future here; *everything* is being created and manifested in the moment.

This realization of eternity's snail-like pace is so daunting, that spirits here give up thoughts of advancement, and focus more fully on living the now. It is time to relax: attempting to progress is considered shortsighted; one becomes satisfied to simply be, and let all take its natural course. Ironically, this proves to be a main way spirit advances here.

"Row, row your boat, *gently down* the stream." (American nursery song)

"Be still, and know that I *am* God: ...." (Psalms 46:10)

"...I will utter things which have been kept secret from the foundation of the world." (Matthew 13:35)

This expansion of duration affects everything in one's universe, including how soul views other souls, and what can be done for them. It introduces a deeper level of detachment. One steps back; a large part of their previous naiveté is simply crushed. It is time to relax with other souls as well; all *is* in place; every soul *is* being saved; God *is* perfect.

Experience is the teacher, and it is difficult to rush the experiences needed to produce realizations, and deeper, more profound realizations, and their application, are what is needed to grow in Christ. One can point the way and help inspire others to go with God, and one can sincerely support every soul within their orbit, but very little can ever be taught; in addition, realizations and wisdom cannot be transferred from one soul to another. If indeed they could be, God would simply make all souls realized.

As it is, God's love has created the lower heavens as a process whereby soul can become realized, and experience the very deepest of joys.

A second major area of realization in this heaven concerns power, its origin, its use, and its surrender. Power makes everything in creation possible, including love.

"And in very deed for this *cause* have I raised thee up, for to shew *in* thee my power; and that my name may be declared throughout all the earth." (Exodus 9:16)

It may seem counterintuitive, but one learns in this heaven that the way to generate power is by doing nothing: quiet repose, stillness, and contemplative silence generate tremendous power. This power is not personal power, it comes from God.

"God hath spoken once; twice have I heard this; that power *belongeth* to God." (Psalms 62:11)

"And Balaam said unto Balak, Lo, I am come unto thee: have I now any power at all to say anything? The word that God putteth in my mouth, that shall I speak." (Numbers 22:38)

All use of this power is surrendered to God. One channels it but does not wield it. Christ determines when and how to use this power through one.

"God *is* my strength and power: and he maketh my way perfect." (II Samuel 22:33)

"Let every soul be subject unto the higher powers. For there is no power but of God: the powers that be are ordained of God." (Romans 13:1)

"For the kingdom of God *is* not in word, but in power." (I Corinthians 4:20)

When one's spirit progresses to the top of this heaven, they join an infinite ocean of realized souls that have become sons/daughters of God. There is no way to describe this sea of love, power, wisdom and freedom; it is beyond all conception, and spirit has returned to its original heaven and departure point; the prodigal son/daughter is finally home, after a journey that could not be measured in time; it has reached the top of Jacob's ladder, become one with Christ, and is now a realized "Lord of Heaven."

This is the ultimate exaltation, deification, and apotheosis of spirit, and is the eventual home of all creation. Jacob's ladder is in reality an escalator, and all creation is on it. Soul seeks its Creator; God draws them home, and saves *every* last sheep in the fold.

"How think ye? If a man have an hundred sheep, and one of them be gone astray, doth he not leave the ninety and nine, and goeth into the mountains, and seeketh that which is gone astray? And if so be that he find it, verily I say unto you, he rejoiceth more of that *sheep,* than of the ninety and nine which went not astray. Even so it is not the will of your Father which is in heaven, that one of these little ones should perish." (Matthew 18:12-14)

"But as many as received him, to them gave he power to become the sons of God, *even* to them that believe on his name: which were born, not of blood, nor of the will of the flesh, nor of the will of man, but of God." (John 1:12)

"Verily, verily, I say unto you, He that believeth on me, the works that I do shall he do also; and greater *works* than these shall he do; because I go unto my father." (John 14:12)

"Jesus said, He who will drink from my mouth will become like me. I myself shall become he, and the things that are hidden will be revealed to him." (Gospel of St. Thomas #108)

There is a viewing of oneself that occurs when one reaches the seventh heaven that is completely unique; it occurs on the physical plane, and one is stunned to see their own spirit/soul, clothed in light, at a distance from the physical body. One's spirit/self demonstrates its total freedom from any earthly restriction or bodily imprisonment. This is the fifth possible viewing of one's own luminous self, and unlike the others, it is seen by the physical eyes while one is "wide awake."

THE HEART OF GOD

The seventh heaven is the last heaven of manifested creation, but it is not the last heaven. Within the seventh heaven is a dark void *without* light or sound; the contrast to the intensity of the seventh heaven is insane; there is a *great calm* that is wonderful. There are untold levels. This is where the Word emanates from before it manifests in the seventh heaven. This is known as the heart of God, and it is perfectly possible for a spirit to graduate into these regions. Beings here live within their own light; their beauty and light are not imaginable, their numbers are uncountable.

If a spirit does move into these heavens, a sixth viewing of one's *own* luminous essence occurs. One meets Christ within, their "Father." This particular experience dwarfs all previous meetings. All of the viewings of one's luminous selves differ; they each define a higher level of oneself within, and occur at propitious milestones in one's own personal growth.

There is a notable distinction by the disciple St. John, that explains the difference between God, and one's "Father." First, one cannot see God, as God is a spirit.

"No man hath seen God at any time. …." (I John 4:12)

"God is a Spirit: and they that worship him must worship *him* in spirit and in truth." (John 4:24)

However, one *can* see their Father, as viewing one's Christ-Self is perfectly possible. "Not that any man hath seen the Father, save he which is of God, he hath seen the Father." (John 6:46)

"Beloved, now are we the sons of God, and it doth not yet appear what we shall be: but we know that, when he shall appear, we shall be like him; for we shall see him as he is." (I John 3:2)

These viewings of one's luminous selves are supremely important. Each one occurs at a major life-changing initiation, and is a particularly singular experience. They are guideposts helping soul determine where it is in Christ's vast creation, and the individual sees, with their own eyes, the ultimate truth of their own identity. One *must* see it to *believe* it; one *does* see it and *does* believe it.

Christ has promised to manifest to the sincere disciple, and does so in many different ways. Millions of believers over the millenniums can attest to this. Christ does this for *all* creatures.

Spirit never stops growing and evolving, and while the requirements for entering the heart of God are known to be very selective, none the less, that is exactly what Archangels have accomplished within their line of evolution, and what Watchers and Silent Ones have achieved within mankind's line of evolution; there are uncountable legions of these Beings, as there was never a beginning to God's existence and creations.

These spirits help the ALMIGHTY GOD run ITS vast creations. They have gigantic missions and responsibilities. Creation is kept in order by the ABSOLUTE through ITS multitudes of channels, which keep everything perfectly in place. These Silent Watchers and Archangels are not easily understood, and are obsessed with their missions. They have immense freedom and power, and have little to do with individuals. They serve in ecstasy, and are the closest Beings to the ALMIGHTY ABSOLUTE GOD known.

BECOMING CLOSE TO CHRIST

"Wherefore take unto you the whole amour of God, that ye may be able to withstand in the evil day, and having done all, to stand. Stand therefore, having your loins girt about with truth, and having on the breastplate of righteousness; And your feet shod with the preparation of the gospel of peace; Above all, taking the shield of faith, wherewith ye shall be able to quench all the fiery darts of the wicked. And take the helmet of salvation, and the sword of the Spirit, which is the word of God: praying always with all prayer and supplication in the Spirit, …." (Ephesians 6:13-18)

Accepting Christ

"And Jesus said unto them, I am the bread of life: he that cometh to me shall never hunger; and he that believeth on me shall never thirst." (John 6:35)

"Verily, verily, I say unto you, He that heareth my word, and believeth on him that sent me, hath everlasting life, and shall not come unto condemnation; but is passed from death unto life." (John 5:24)

The deeper teachings of Christ are very similar to mainstream Christianity, when it comes to practicing sincere adherence to Christ. Both would agree that the first necessary step is to accept Christ as your personal guide and savior. This will require repentance, which is classically defined as "a change in direction." One has agreed to give up their personal will and mind to Christ, and to follow Him in all things.

This may be the biggest milestone in the life of soul since it began human incarnations; if sincere, they are safe in the arms of Christ, and have completed the first step of salvation.

If the individual is totally and unequivocally committed to accepting Christ, one may see this as a sign that this decision is coming from soul, which has influenced and impressed the mind into agreement with this momentous decision. If on the other hand, this was simply a personality conversion, the decision is in danger of not manifesting in any meaningful way. In spiritual matters, sincerity is the operative characteristic required.

Once the individual has accepted Christ, the journey of *conforming* to Christ begins, and this is perhaps the most difficult adventure that one could attempt; the secret teachings believe that going it alone is next to impossible. One needs help and guidance from a disciple or teacher who has completed this journey. The logical choice for most Christians is Jesus the Christ, the Wonderful Counselor; for others, it may be the Virgin Mary, or a favorite saint.

The secret doctrine believes that there are also others that Christ has designated to help. These are disciple/teachers, who have reached the fifth heaven or higher in their own journey towards becoming a son/daughter of God, and are operating from the first level of the Christ Consciousness, or higher.

An advantage in using one of Christ's disciples from the fifth heaven or above, is that one may find a disciple/teacher presently living in a human body; this can be very helpful. This is rare but does happen; St. Francis of Assisi, is an example of such a channel. The believer would want inner guidance from Christ before trusting a teacher to help them on their journey. There are certain guideposts if one is looking for such an individual.

A realized disciple/teacher is totally ethical and leads a life of demonstrable piety. If teaching others, they do not charge money for their help. If there is a fee it is nominal and very small, perhaps to cover printing costs or such. A disciple/teacher does not live off others, is gainfully employed, and pays his own way in all things.

A qualified disciple/teacher never interferes in one's personal life and does not give commands, or tell a student what to do: they champion freedom. They do *not* have or desire titles, and refuse to take credit for any good thing, knowing that they are but a channel for Christ. They radiate impersonal love and always work for a student's spiritual benefit.

A disciple/teacher from the fifth heaven or higher, can work with the individual on the inner planes of heaven at night, soul to soul: this is immensely helpful, as an instructor of this caliber can teach one all manner of things, while supporting and protecting them.

If one is using a teacher, be it Jesus the Christ, the Virgin Mary, or some other credible holy person, the sincere Christian will meet with their guide in dreams and visions on the Astral Plane, and higher; Christ will manifest to them. This is happening to millions of sincere followers all over the globe, and in every heaven in existence.

"He that hath my commandments, and keepeth them, he it is that loveth me: and he that loveth me shall be loved of my father, and I will love him, and will manifest myself to him." (John 14:21)

If one is considering using a disciple/teacher for help, Christ will give His approval in a dream, vision, or some other clear communicative manner; this is a given. Furthermore, a relationship with a teacher should enable a student over time to become totally independent of *any* outside instruction, and lean completely on their *own* inner guidance from Christ; self-direction is one of Christ's primary goals; He wants one to be a free, independent son/daughter of God, a spiritual adult that is their own priest in Christ.

"But the anointing ye have received of him abideth in you, and ye need not that any man teach you: but as the same anointing teacheth you of all things, and is truth, and is no lie, and even as it has taught you, ye shall abide in him." (I John 2:27)

"But be not ye called Rabbi: for one is your master, *even* Christ; and all ye are brethren. And call no *man* your father upon the earth: for one is your Father, which is in heaven. Neither be ye called masters: for one is your Master, *even* Christ." (Matthew 23:8-10)

Before deciding to accept Christ, it is wise to consider what this gigantic, life-changing decision entails. Christ in Jesus set out qualifications to be found worthy of Christ; they may be challenging to fully comply with.

"Jesus said, 'I disclose my mysteries to those (who are worthy) of (my) mysteries. Do not let your left hand know what your right hand is doing." (Gospel of St. Thomas #62)

"He that loveth father or mother more than me is not worthy of me: and he that loveth son or daughter more than me is not worthy of me. And he that taketh not his cross, and followeth after me, is not worthy of me." (Matthew 10:37-38)

The secret teachings believe that taking up the cross and following Christ, means giving up one's personal ego, mind, and will to Christ, and being crucified with Him. The crucifixion will occur as one purifies their mind and emotions, atoning for past indiscretions, sin, and negative karma; simultaneously, one learns and applies wonderful lessons gleaned from such trials.

"Knowing this, that our old man is crucified with *him*, that the body of sin might be destroyed, that henceforth we should not serve sin." (Romans 6:6)

The deeper teachings do not believe one is born in sin, although they do believe in karma that has been created in previous lifetimes. However, many are born with very positive karma. Sin may be defined as when one does not do what they believe is right. There are those who *always* do what they believe is right.

"Be ye therefore perfect, even as your Father which is in heaven is perfect." (Matthew 5:48)

These requirements to be found worthy of Christ are not necessarily simple or easy, and they may require years of work to fully honor them. Those who ignore these considerations, and are not sincere in attempting to implement a Christ-like life, run the risk of being found unworthy.

"Not every one that saith unto me, Lord, Lord, shall enter into the kingdom of heaven; but he that doeth the will of my Father which is in heaven. Many will say to me in that day, Lord, Lord, have we not prophesied in thy name? and in thy name have cast out devils? and in thy name done many wonderful works? And then will I profess unto them, I never knew you: depart from me, ye that work iniquity." (Matthew 7:21-23)

Commitment

Once one has made the quintessential decision to accept Christ, the success of their journey will depend on their level of commitment. Are they all in, or is it merely a social conversion, or something in between. The deeper teachings of Christ believe that to have profound experiences with Christ, one *must* be a fanatic. One *must* want it, and want it very badly, and for a very long time. It *must* become a way of life.

"And ye shall seek me, and find *me,* when ye shall search for me with all your heart." (Jeramiah 29:13)

Every level of commitment to Christ is honored; however, to those who go totally all the way, making Christ their everything, they are blessed with the deepest and most electrifying experiences with Christ known to man. This spiritual fanaticism is an *inner* quality and not observable by others; it is a preoccupation with Christ inside oneself. It *is* the treasure of their heart, the love of their life, the sum of their desire, their pearl of price.

In becoming familiar with what Christ asks one to do, it becomes clear that a full commitment to Christ is required to be fully successful. Halfway measures, or splitting spiritual goals with worldly goals, is not going to succeed. To be successful at attaining full salvation, and *have experiences* with Christ, one is going to have to be singularly focused. This is made clear time and again in the holy gospel:

"No man can serve two masters: for either he will hate the one, and love the other; or else he will hold to the one, and despise the other. Ye cannot serve God and mammon." (Matthew 6:24)

"For where your treasure is, there will your heart be also." (Matthew 6:21)

"Who, when he had found one pearl of great price, went and sold all that he had, and bought it." (Matthew 13:46)

"Pray without ceasing." (I Thessalonians 5:17)

"And he said, The human one is like a wise fisherman who cast his net into the sea and drew it up from the sea full of little fish. Among them the wise fisherman discovered a large fine fish. He threw all the little fish back into the sea, and easily chose the large fish. Anyone here with two good ears better listen." (Gospel of St. Thomas #8)

"Jesus said, A person cannot mount two horses or bend two bows. And a slave cannot serve two masters, otherwise that slave will honor the one and offend the other." (Gospel of St. Thomas #47)

"God is either of supreme importance, or no importance at all." (Rabbi Hillel)

"Jesus said unto him, Thou shalt love the Lord thy God with all thy heart, and with all thy soul, and with all thy mind." (Matthew 22:37)

A question at this point might be: What does total commitment look like? The secret doctrine might suggest something loosely similar to the following: devotions three or more times a day; daily study of the scriptures and other helpful works; semi-constant prayer and communion with Christ; listening to the audible Word; working on transforming one's mind; possible discussions with like believers; and, being open to being a channel for Christ at all times. The goal is full salvation, the mind of Christ, and the Christ consciousness.

One does not have to forfeit worldly responsibilities to do this; to the contrary, one's life begins to take on greater order, and one's duties are handled in a more fulfilling, responsible manner.

Many will question this, and say that due to family responsibilities and work, they do not have the time for such a schedule. This may or may not be true. Devotions do not have to be long and time consuming. Fifteen minutes for some devotions is plenty of time to connect with Christ, and most believers may have time before getting out of bed in the morning, possibly before work, during lunch time, after work, in the evening before bed, and in bed before going to sleep. Does one have time for God?

In addition, many have jobs where one's attention can be elsewhere at times. Admittedly, there *are* those that literally are so engaged in their mission that they have little time for devotions; their entire life is a devotion.

Spiritual commitment is best done in *small* steps and not all at once. Perhaps one begins with devotions in the morning for twenty minutes. Maybe after a time, one adds devotions at the end of the day. Hopefully, one has found something to study and contemplate that speaks to them, and that they can apply to their Christian life. The point is not to keep expanding the amount of time in devotions; the point is to gradually look at things the way Christ does.

After practicing careful listening, remembering that the music of the Word is very faint in the beginning, one may begin to hear the audible sounds of the Holy Spirit. The first sound heard is often like the single high note of a flute. If one cannot hear it at first, one might listen to the silence, and ask Christ for help in hearing His voice. It may be so faint in the beginning that one wonders if they are really hearing it.

One does *not* drop out of the world, or one's worldly responsibilities; instead, one gradually spiritualizes the consciousness, and begins looking at the world with a more transcendent, spiritual *viewpoint*. Ironically, staying in contact with Christ will give one much more energy and poise to deal with one's worldly duties. In addition, they will begin interacting with their everyday life in a new and improved way, finding love, peace and joy. Devotions allow Christ to energize one; a valence is established.

"Jesus said, Come to me, for my yoke is comfortable and my lordship is gentle, and you will find rest for yourselves." (Gospel of St. Thomas #90)

"Casting all your care upon him; for he careth for you." (I Peter 5:7)

"This book of the law shall not depart out of thy mouth: but thou shall meditate therein day and night, that thou mayest observe to do according to all that is written therein: for then shalt thou make thy way prosperous, and then shalt thou have good success." (Joshua 1:8)

"Thou will keep *him* in perfect peace *whose* mind *is* stayed *on thee*: because he trusteth in thee." (Isaiah 26:3)

If one follows through with their daily devotions and study, proving to Christ that they are sincerely committed, after a period of time, perhaps in a handful of months or sooner, one will begin to have experiences with their higher self, and Christ.

The spiritual happenings will begin with little things, so as to prevent spiritual shock, and often times, one may think that a spiritual occurrence is either their imagination or coincidence; however, the experiences will gradually increase in magnitude and scope, and it is not long before the believer sees the beginning of a communicative relationship with the higher self, the Holy Spirit, and Christ; this occurs through hearing the Word, dreams, visions, signs, flashes, intuition, and other unique forms of communication.

This becomes extremely exciting, and begins making Christ *real*, increasing one's fervor for further study and devotional practices. In addition, one's devotions become an oasis of peace, bliss, love, and wisdom, and one's spiritual love nature awakens. A profound experience with Christ sets one's spiritual hair ablaze; these indescribable events are enjoyed by the those that are totally committed, and it *is* presently occurring all over the entire globe, and beyond, in all of the heavens.

"He that hath my commandments, and keepeth them, he it is that loveth me: and he that loveth me shall be loved of my father, and I will love him, and will manifest myself to him." (John 14:21)

There are endless antitheses in the successful believers' spiritual journey: one acts much, to be action less; one *gives* their all, to let Christ *do* it all; one becomes nothing, to become everything; stop thinking, to know everything; one must die to live.

"For to me to live *is* Christ, and to die *is* gain." (Philippians 1:21)

Study

"Study to shew thyself approved unto God, a workman that needeth not to be ashamed, rightly dividing the word of truth." (II Timothy 2:13)

"Apply thine heart unto instruction, and thine ears to the words of knowledge." (Proverbs 23:12)

Study is one of the important components to a successful Christian life. The main topic of study is one's life, as one engages in a deep self-analysis of their thoughts and actions, attempting to conform their life to Christ's direction. For most Christians in this day and age, study also includes the printed word, although many who have reached full salvation in the past were illiterate, especially during the time of Jesus the Christ. Today, in addition to the Holy Bible, there is a vast selection of wonderful books and aids that can help one's Christian practice.

Generally, study materials can be loosely divided into two categories: the first category deals with spiritual information, facts and figures, the second centers on life experiences, realizations, and awareness. In the first category, one may learn the facts of Jesus the Christ's life, memorize verses in the Holy Bible, or study the process of soul's growth.

For example, some students of the secret teachings are drawn to the study of soul's evolution, throughout the long journey towards Christ. There are wonderful books that explain this in incredible detail, especially the voluminous texts of Christian Theosophy, Hinduism, Buddhism, and Sikhism.

A second example might be those who outline the Holy Bible, and can detail the history of the various prophets in the Old Testament, or chronicle the events in the life of Jesus the Christ. Others may study the lives of the saints, or perhaps include a study and knowledge of the Eastern religions, which have thousands of profound volumes available.

While these pursuits are laudable and somewhat beneficial, they are not what the deeper teachings favor: facts, figures, and a knowledge of spiritual events advance soul but little; those following the secret doctrine pursue *higher states of consciousness, realizations, spiritual experiences,* and a *deeper level of awareness,* not factual information. One could memorize the entire Holy Bible and not advance in Christ one iota.

One's *level of awareness* and their *actions,* determine which heaven the believer belongs in, not what information they may have studied or memorized. Consequently, it is the second category of study which is held to be more profitable; this includes an analysis of one's life, and the contemplation and realization of the spiritual principles governing one's actions and beliefs.

Most of the guidance and direction in the second kind of study, comes from *inside* one during prayer, study, and devotions, and is not dependent on an *outside* source. This not only increases the *understanding* and *realization* of Christian principles, but increases one's overall *awareness* as well. This results in higher states of consciousness and spiritually refined actions, bringing the Christian closer to Christ.

An important reason for study is to *understand* how the Holy Spirit operates, and what its motives and principles are. This will aid in fielding and understanding Christ's guidance. Sometimes this guidance is hard to understand, and counter to what one has previously been led to believe. Several examples of this may be helpful.

For instance, one constantly hears prayers for world peace and goodwill among nations; while this is naturally desirable, Christ has a different approach in the lower heavens: He promotes and instigates war and strife. God cares about souls and their growth, not bodies and personalities.

"Think not that I am come to send peace on earth: I came not to send peace, but a sword." (Matthew 10:34)

Human personalities and bodies do not go to heaven; it is soul that is climbing Jacob's ladder.

"Now this I say, brethren, that flesh and blood cannot inherit the kingdom of God; …." (I Corinthians 15:50)

War promotes spiritual experiences and realizations, suffering and repentance, religion and spirituality, individuality and wisdom; God is appealed to. Peace promotes conformity and stagnation, worldliness and hedonism, selfishness and indulgence, and a deep thanklessness that takes things for granted; God is forgotten.

Christ's motive on this level is to provide experiences that impel soul to realize the truth. The goal is *inner* peace, "which passeth all understanding"; outer peace is secondary and may not be as spiritually profitable.

"Jesus said, Men think, perhaps, that it is peace which I have come to cast upon the world. They do not know that it is dissension which I have come to cast upon the earth: fire, sword, and war.…" (Gospel of St. Thomas #16)

A second example of how the Holy Spirit operates contrary to conventional belief, is found in Jesus the Christ's teaching on the family. To many Christians, family is everything. Jesus sometimes is critical towards family, and warns people not to love their family more than God. It is known that he refused to see his own family and friends, when they planned "to lay hold on him" to stop him from preaching, claiming "He is beside himself." (Mark 3:21) They thought He was crazy.

"And the multitude sat about him, Behold, thy mother and thy brethren without seek for thee. And he answered them saying, Who is my mother or my brethren? And he looked round about on them which sat about him, and said, Behold, my mother and my brethren! For whosoever shall do the will of God, the same is my brother, and my sister, and mother." (Mark 3:32-35)

"And a man's foes *shall be* they of his own household. He that loveth father or mother more than me is not worthy of me: and he that loveth son or daughter more than me is not worthy of me." (Matthew 10:36-38)

"If any *man* come to me, and hate not his father, and mother, and wife, and children, and brethren, and sisters, yea, and his own life also, he cannot be my disciple." (Luke 14:26)

And what about Christ's teaching on family harmony and love?

"For I come to set a man at variance against his father, and the daughter against her mother, and the daughter in law against her mother in law." (Matthew 10:35)

The secret teachings believe that Christ desires independent self-directed individuals, that are relying solely on their own inner authority. That individuality is prized by Christ is self-evident; no two people are remotely alike, nor do they fully agree; even identical twins are often opposites.

Christ does not want cloned conformists that follow others like sheep, lean on others for advice, and rely on group-think. Christ wants believers to be free and follow Him *inside* themselves. This *may* be one reason for the variance and strife he promised to bring to families and nations, as it forces learning and independence. It definitely gets people off the spiritual couch.

It is evident that family is very important and requires deep, personal love, but its importance is relative; perhaps Christ desires that one sees it in its proper perspective; the relationship with one's spiritual Father is much more important.

To put it into further perspective, the protected doctrine believes that one has been a member of uncountable families, as soul has lived and evolved for eternities; one's extended family may include zillions, and not just on Earth. In the kingdom of heaven, everyone is family with the same Father.

A third notable example of differences between mainstream conventional beliefs, and the hidden teachings, concern the concept of Satan. The deeper doctrine believes that Satan is one's own mind, and is one's main opponent to spiritual truth, especially in the beginning of one's spiritual journey. Until retrained, the mind wants its programmed desires, and it wants them very badly. It is painfully ironic that humanity believes their mind to be the soul. "Because the carnal mind *is* enmity against God: for it is not subject to the law of God, neither indeed can be. So then they that are in the flesh cannot please God." (Romans 8:7-8)

The idea that some evil force could oppose God is not reasonable or logical; it is a subterfuge to protect people from facing their own responsibility for evil. All evil comes from man, not from some angry archangel, and certainly not from God. All powers are from God, including those destructive powers that mankind does not understand, and is fearful of.

"Let every soul be subject to the higher powers. For there is no power but of God: the powers that be are ordained of God." (Romans 13:1)

There are differences between what the priest craft is teaching, and what Christ taught to his disciples. One of these differences, would include the conventional belief that forgiveness of evil deeds is possible through petition, confession, prayer, or monetary indulgences: the fact that Christians suffer incredible tragedy and suffering, should point to the fact that they are atoning for something. They are reaping what they have sown. Nor is the idea that God is testing one scripturally accurate.

"Let no man say when he is tempted, I am tempted of God: for God cannot be tempted with evil, neither tempteth he any man: But every man is tempted, when he is drawn away of his own lust, and enticed. Then when lust hath conceived, it bringeth forth sin: and sin, when it is finished, bringeth forth death." (James 1:13-15)

Christ is clear, one reaps what they sow; every human being either knows this or senses it. What goes around comes around. No person gets away with anything; both good and bad karma come back precisely as warranted, and this perfectly exact system plays out over lifetimes; God is perfectly just; Christ is perfectly just; both are also divinely merciful or no one would be saved.

It is not as if some angel is handing out rewards and punishments: one's very own creations fashion an effect in the spiritual ethers that returns to them; it is exact. Bad things do not happen to good people; they do happen to good people who have been bad.

In addition, the deeper teachings do not believe in a hell where souls are sent forever, or that all Christians go to the same heaven for eternity, or that verbal salvation is viable, or that children are a blank slate and innocent.

These examples of differences between conventional belief, and what the secret teachings believe is a deeper truth, are but a small sampling, but it is meant to highlight one reason for spiritual study; there is a deeper layer to Christ's teaching that is counterintuitive to the average believer, *and,* to the deepest disciple in Christ; this is, and always will be the case; there is no end to growth in Christ; deep truth keeps getting deeper…eternally. This *is* absolute.

This is not a criticism of conventional Christianity, as there are multiple levels of truth within Christianity, that are tailored to numerous levels of growth. Daily study of the Word and other resonant truth, can uncover deeper layers of meaning to those who earnestly seek it, with guidance from the living Christ. There are many deep secrets and mysteries.

"Jesus said, It is to those who are worthy of my mysteries that I tell my mysteries. Do not let your left (hand) know what your right (hand) is doing." (Gospel of St. Thomas #62)

"And he said, unto you it is given to know the mysteries of the kingdom of God: but to others in parables; that seeing they might not see, and hearing they might not understand." (Luke 8:10)

"Jesus said, Let him who seeks continue seeking until he finds. When he finds, he will become troubled. When he becomes troubled, he will be astonished, and he will rule over the All." (Gospel of St. Thomas #2)

A study of spiritual truth will also spiritualize the consciousness, and answer many of the numerous questions that every sincere follower has. After a time, it becomes a blissful staple of one's devotional practices. The more attention that the individual puts on spiritual viewpoints, the less attention is available to put on the world. Old ways of thinking, and desires for worldly gratification, gradually die a natural death, as there is less and less attention available to keep them alive. A question at this point may be: What might be the best way to study?

Devotions

"But his delight *is* in the law of the Lord; and in his law doth he meditate day and night. And he shall be like a tree planted by the rivers of water, that bringeth forth his fruit in his season; his leaf also shall not wither; and whatsoever he doeth shall prosper." (Psalms 1:1-3)

From an esoteric point of view, there is a sequence of steps in the successful Christian life that leads to total fulfillment and success, no matter the level or capacity of the person involved; it is universally true.

The first step is to sincerely repent, (a change in direction) and accept Christ as your savior and guide, agreeing to let this power run one's life. The second step is to commit oneself to daily devotions and study, multiple times a day.

After a few months or earlier, the third step occurs; one begins to have experiences with Christ. At first, they are little things, and one may not be sure if they are spiritual occurrences or coincidence; however, the experiences become larger, perhaps a clear spiritual dream or an unmistakable sign.

This creates the fourth step: the Christian journey with Christ becomes *real;* it is no longer an imaginative mental concept. This leads to the fifth step: one begins to see what the Holy Spirit is doing for one, and subsequently, falls in love with Christ. This gradually creates the sixth step, joy and fulfillment. This sequence of steps is powered by multiple daily devotions.

"Draw nigh to God, and he will draw nigh to you." (James 4:8)

Among the many kinds of devotions, the deeper secret teachings of Christ favor spiritual contemplation, not only as the best way to study, but the best way to directly obtain guidance and communication from Christ; this comes through one's own spirit and soul. There is a major reason for this preference, as spiritual contemplation combines focused thinking, and stillness; stillness involves not thinking, or the absence of thought.

As noted previously, the mind cannot *think* of guidance from Christ; it must *receive* it from the Lord. This demands the utmost in one's receptivity. Consequently, the mind must be still, as thinking blocks inner communication with the higher self, the Holy Spirit and Christ.

"Be still, and know that I *am* God." (Psalms 46:10)

Correctly performed meditation, which differs markedly from contemplation, is the absence of all thought; however, many find this extremely difficult, especially among Western Christians, who are used to their mind racing the entire time they are awake. The secret way believes that meditation is too passive, and not the proper balance of being and nonbeing, action and non-action.

Additionally, prolonged meditation is not natural to man, and it is believed by the deeper teachings, that all interaction between God and man should be perfectly natural. Sometimes, in the beginning of one's spiritual journey, meditation is recommended to slow down the mind somewhat, before the believer turns to spiritual contemplation.

There are many terms denoting or connoting contemplation. Five of them in the Holy Bible are stillness, muse, ponder, meditate and trance. At the time of the King James translation, contemplation was not yet used as a word, and their use of the word "meditate," is how one uses contemplate today.   One cannot "meditate" on something, or technically, one is contemplating.

Other words or phrases used today include: consider; reflect; mull over; weigh; deliberate; ruminate; speculate; brood over; chew over; kick around; envisage; reckon; and foresee. They all refer to a combination of focused thinking, combined with pauses in thinking.

It is during the short pauses in thinking that the higher self, the Holy Spirit, and Christ, send their guidance, insights, and realizations. These communications are usually fast and subtle; one must be ready to receive them. This takes some practice, as they show up suddenly through intuition, and might not seem that different from other thoughts. However, they arrive with a particular kind of presence, that some describe as having had something laid on their heart, or fielding a particular feeling.

Most people contemplate much of the day about the daily things of life, whether it be their family, friends, finances, health, work, or anything else that arises. It is perfectly natural, and the only difference with spiritual contemplation is what one places their attention on to contemplate.

The first subject to contemplate during devotions, is usually any major challenge one may be facing. If one is alone without distractions, still and relaxed, quietly asking the Lord for guidance, and reflecting on what is troubling them, they will get answers. The correct solution from Christ usually carries with it a feeling of spiritual correctness, and it is often something one has not previously thought of. It may arrive as a major epiphany, or a quiet feeling of rightness.

Guidance received from within may provoke the mind's defensiveness, and it may require subjugation of the ego. For example, one may be rightfully due an apology, but instead, is led by the Holy Spirit to give one to the offending party.

If one is not still but restless, attempting to *think* of an answer, their mind will play ping pong between various viewpoints of the problem, first from one side and then the other side, thinking in a circle and unable to make a decision.

If one is not facing a challenge in their life that needs guidance, one's spiritual life makes an effective topic for one's devotions. For example, it may be about where one feels they are in their Christian life, or perhaps what their mission here on Earth may entail. At times, one may revisit some situation during the day that created a slight disturbance in the "force," or a feeling that something could have been better handled. Sometimes, the Lord will bring a topic to mind that needs attention.

If one is satisfied on where they feel they are with Christ, and have already given the big questions ample attention, scripture and other profound literature are great subjects to contemplate. Anything that is speaking to one is perfect, whether it is a verse in Matthew, or a self-help book that has provided useful suggestions.

Often times, it is a particular verse or point that resonates with one, and provides the basis for a longer examination. It is useful to focus contemplation on a worthy topic; however, at other times, soul may spontaneously take one through many disparate considerations. None the less, usually one wants to focus on a spiritual subject, or it is easy to find oneself contemplating day to day trivia. For example, one may pick a special verse to reflect on, like John 14:12:

"Verily, verily, I say unto you, He that beliveth on me, the works that I do shall he do also; and greater *works* than these shall he do; because I go unto my Father."

This verse is loaded with profound points to consider and examine, especially worthy of much reflection. From an esoteric point of view, several conclusions may arise when contemplating this verse:

1. The fact that Jesus begins with the words, "Verily, verily," means that He is strongly emphasizing the point that He is about to make; this truth will be very important.
2. The word "believeth" carries and deserves an expanded definition. In the King James version of the Holy Bible, unlike today, believe means much more than a simple belief: if one cleaves to Christ, relies on Him, adheres to His commands, trusts Him, follows Him, loves Him, worships Him, *then*, one is *believing*.
3. Christ Jesus uses the word "shall" twice, indicating the future. The disciples and others who believe in Christ are not doing works like Christ Jesus is doing now, but *shall* in the future. This indicates a progression of growth, that those who follow Jesus the Christ will someday be like Him, and be doing the same works that He is performing. They are climbing Jacob's ladder.
4. Christ Jesus goes even further with the second *shall*, saying that someday those who *believe* in Him, will do even greater works than He has done. This also confirms that there is a continuation of growth to glorious heights, as believers will do even greater things that Christ Jesus has presently demonstrated. Over long cycles of time, souls eventually climb to the very top of Jacob's ladder.
5. This second use of *shall* is staggering, because it promises future parity with Jesus as He is now. Someday, believers shall be as He is presently, and some day, they will be even greater than that. Jesus also will have continued growing; there is *never* an end to growth.

"Beloved, now are we the sons of God, and it doth not yet appear what we shall be: but we know that, when he shall appear, we shall be like him; for we shall see him as he is." (I John 3:2)

The last phrase of the verse appears to indicate two things; first, that the disciples will, in some small way, be taking the place of Christ Jesus, since He is shortly leaving to be with His Father; secondly, Christ Jesus is foretelling His death and resurrection.

These possible conclusions are head-twisters, and many Christians may struggle to believe them, yet these viewpoints are not stretching the verse or its interpretation; these truths are spoken by Christ Jesus as literal, declarative statements. He is foretelling that sincere believers *will someday* be as He *is,* a son of God. This interpretation is also at the very heart of the difference between the deeper secret teachings, and mainstream Christianity.

"But as many as received him, to them gave he power to become the sons of God, *even* to them that believe on his name: Which were born, not of blood, nor of the will of the flesh, nor of the will of man, but of God." (John 1:12)

"Jesus said, He who will drink from my mouth will become like me. I myself shall become he, and the things that are hidden shall be revealed to him." (Gospel of St. Thomas #108)

"The Jews answered him, saying, For a good work we stone thee not; but for blasphemy; and because that thou, being a man, makest thyself God. Jesus answered them, Is it not written in your law, I said, Ye are Gods? If he called them gods, unto whom the word of God came, and the scripture cannot be broken; Say ye of him, whom the Father hath sanctified, and sent into the world, Thou blasphemest; because I said, I am the son of God?" (John 10:33-36)

The purpose of spiritual contemplation is to establish contact with Christ through one's own soul and spirit, and field profound guidance, insights and realizations from within. If one can bring intermittent stillness and the absence of thought into their devotions, they will be setting the stage for direct communications from Christ; illumination comes from waiting upon the Lord.

Once the believer can recognize guidance from Christ, be it a dream, the audible Word, a feeling, a flash, or some other kind of messaging, they are in an extremely advantageous position: not to minimize this, but all they have to do is follow their guidance. The believer will *know* what to do. The Wonderful Counselor has taken over and one can hear *His* voice.

"Verily, verily, I say unto you, the hour is coming, and now is, when the dead shall hear the voice of the son of God: and they that hear shall live." (John 5:25)

Prayer

Prayer is direct communion with Christ; it may be done anywhere, by anyone, at any time. Christ in Jesus instructs one on how to pray, and where to pray, and He exemplifies His teaching, through constant prayer to His Father.

Christ Jesus teaches believers to pray alone in secret, and He Himself is regularly seeking out places to pray alone.

"And when thou prayest, thou shalt not be as the hypocrites *are:* for they love to pray in the synagogues and in the corners of the streets, that they may be seen of men. Verily I say unto you, They have their reward. But thou, when thou prayest, enter into thy closet, and when thou hast shut thy door, pray to thy Father which is in secret; and thy Father which seeth in secret shall reward thee openly." (Matthew 6:5-6)

"And in the morning, rising up a great while before day, he went out, and departed into a solitary place, and there prayed." (Mark 1:35)

"And he withdrew himself into the wilderness, and prayed." (Luke 5:16)

"And when he had sent them away, he departed into a mountain to pray." (Mark 6:46)

"And it came to pass in those days, that he went out into a mountain to pray, and continued all night in prayer to God." (Luke 6:12)

Christ Jesus also instructs believers how *not* to pray:

"But when ye pray, use not vain repetitions, as the heathen *do:* for they think they shall be heard for their much speaking." (Matthew 6:7)

"Beware of the scribes, which desire to walk in long robes, and love greetings in the markets, and the highest seats in the synagogues, and the chief rooms at feasts; Which devour widows' houses, and for a shew make long prayers: the same shall receive greater damnation." (Luke 20:46)

It is a source of humor, that church leaders today completely ignore these instructions by Christ Jesus. They are the same individuals as existed in Jesus' time.

Christ Jesus cautions believers not to forget prayers for those whom are against one: "But I say unto you, Love your enemies, bless them that curse you, do good to them that hate you, and pray for them which despitefully use you, and persecute you; ...." (Matthew 5:44)

In addition, when praying, Christ asks one to forgive those who have wronged one: "And when ye stand praying, forgive, if ye have ought against any: that your Father also which is in heaven may forgive you your trespasses." (Mark 11:25)

Christ Jesus gives believers a most wonderful prayer to recite:
"After this manner therefore pray ye:
Our father which art in heaven, Hallowed be thy name.
Thy kingdom come. Thy will be done in earth, as *it is* in heaven. Give us this day our daily bread.
And forgive us our debts, as we forgive our debtors.
And lead us not into temptation, but deliver us from evil:
For thine is the kingdom and the power, and the glory, forever. Amen." (Matthew 6:9-13)

Perhaps the ultimate prayer is to pray for God's will:
"Be not ye therefore like unto them: for your Father knoweth what things ye have need of, before ye ask him." (Matthew 6:8)

"And he went a little further, and fell on his face, and prayed, saying, O my Father, if it be possible, let this cup pass from me: nevertheless not as I will, but as thou wilt." (Matthew 26:39)

A question at this point may be: What besides God's will, is it OK to pray *for?*

The secret teachings believe that it is perfectly fine to pray for *all* needs, whatever they may be; Christ provides everything without exception. In addition, do not forget to believe that they will be received.

"And all things, whatsoever ye shall ask in prayer, believing, ye shall receive." (Matthew 21:22)

"Thou openest thy hand, and satisfiest the desire of every living thing." (Psalm 145:16)

Short prayers are also an effective way to connect with Christ; sometimes these are called *mantras*, or repetitions. Phrases such as "I love you Father," "help me Father," or "thank you Father," can be so very helpful when repeated a number of times. One can also use phrases that are specifically designed for a circumstance or problem, and if one keeps repeating them for some time, they have a way of sinking in.

For example, if one is having a difficult time forgiving a person for a terrible wrong committed against themselves, one might say, "Father, help me forgive," one hundred times. If this has not registered, another hundred.

The deeper hidden teachings believe that one is praying to Christ *inside* one, *outside one,* and *as* one. St. Paul explains this, although in a somewhat circular way. First, he states that the mystery of the ages has been revealed: "… which is Christ in you, the hope of glory: …." (Colossians 1:27)

Secondly, he writes that "…Christ *is* all, and in all." (Colossians 3:11)

The inescapable conclusion is that one *is* Christ; there is nothing else that soul, spirit, or *anything* else can be. One's self is a cell of the body of Christ; the hidden teachings believe that man's divine self *is* Christ, and one's *true* Father.

"All things were made by him; and without him was not anything made that was made." (John 1:3)

"I and *my* Father are one." (John 10:30)

Consequently, one is not only praying to Christ outside oneself; Christ, and the kingdom of God, are within one as well. (Luke 17:21)

In addition, they *are* one.

Listening

Simply *listening* has a special place within the deepest secret teachings, as this doctrine believes that the Holy Word of God can be heard from within. This is not as unknown or strange as some might believe, as several of the world religions feature the practice of listening to these melodies, especially various schools of Hinduism, Buddhism, Sikhism, and the right-hand path of *Tantra*. There are also several American paths that emphasize this devotional practice: MasterPath; *Radha Soami; Ruhani Satsang,* Eckankar, and others.

Jesus the Christ makes clear reference to the fact that it can be heard, when he states that the Holy Spirit is like the coming and going of the wind, and declares that those born of the spirit can hear it. (John 3:8)

In the beginning, it can be difficult to hear these sounds; usually, they are faint and very high. At first, it is common to hear a single note, much like a flute. The hidden teachings believe that the effects of listening to these songs are spiritually magical.

One of the primary effects of listening to these notes, is that it introduces stillness; one is not thinking; this is the perfect state to be in for contact with Christ. It is also an easy way to go to sleep. These frequencies are simply the Holy Spirit going through one's consciousness centers (chakras).

A second effect of listening to this music, is that it seems to clean out the mind, in that negative thoughts and emotions seem to fade, and gradually disappear: permanently.

In addition, wonderful realizations and epiphanies occur... effortlessly.

Soul can travel on these currents of the Holy Spirit, as though they were a freeway; this river of life connects with every soul, and with every place throughout the seven heavens; in addition, it *is* every soul and every place.

It is difficult to verbally describe the wonderful effects this practice produces: one would need much larger, all-inclusive words. One is listening to the Holy Spirit of God directly; this holy river of light and sound creates everything, is everything, sustains everything, and is white hot with an all-encompassing love that defies measure. This emanation from God is also man's true identity.

It is not long before the listener will hear many streams of this musical river continuously. Soul will also begin to use it to communicate with one, by increasing its volume at precisely timed moments, or by strongly impressing the mind and emotions. This is *direct communication* with the Holy Word. The secret teachings believe that this communicative relationship with the Holy Spirit is necessary to be born of the spirit, and enter into the kingdom of heaven.

"Jesus answered, Verily, verily, I say unto thee, Except a man be born of water and *of* the Spirit, he cannot enter into the kingdom of God." (John 3:5)

Love

"He that loveth not knoweth not God; for God is love." (I John 4:8)

"And we have known and believed the love that God hath to us. God is love; and he that dwelleth in love dwelleth in God, and God in him." (I John 4:16)

"Jesus said onto him, Thou shalt love the Lord thy God with all thy heart, and with all thy soul, and with all thy mind. This is the first and great commandment. And the second *is* like unto it, Thou shalt love thy neighbor as thyself. On these two commandments hang all the law and the prophets." (Matthew 22:37-40)

Love is the keystone of the successful Christian journey; it is the power that connects one with Christ, and there is no other force that can do this. This presents a challenge for many Christians as they struggle with *how* to love Christ. There is an antidote to this situation that naturally eliminates this problem: experiences with Christ.

One cannot make themselves love something; they must have reasons to love; this is what devotions with Christ create. After months of multiple devotions daily, one *will* begin to *experience* Christ. Many of these experiences will be profound, and they will grow in scope and intensity. These experiences are characterized by an overwhelming love that leaves the recipient awestruck; one *knows* that they are from God.

This activates one's own love nature, and one's Christian journey becomes alive with spiritual passion and love thrills. The idea that miraculous things could only happen during the time of Jesus the Christ is patently false; Christly miracles are *always* occurring to those that deeply love Christ; it is funny that people ask for miracles, when every single thing in life *is* a miracle.

Deep love is pregnant with energy, and this energy polarizes one to their goal. It is like a powerful magnet that attracts the very thing it is focused on. Without this force of intense love, one's Christian journey is lifeless; it is missing the power needed to deeply connect with soul, spirit, and Christ. There is absolutely no alternative to this requirement: it is either full-blown love, or a relationship with Christ in name only.

Many have debated whether love for Christ, and Christ's love for man, is personal or impersonal. Some describe Christ's love with the Greek word *agape,* which is defined as an impersonal, charitable kind of love that Christ has for the church and believers. The secret teachings disagree with that description, and would suggest, that this love affair with Christ is *exceedingly* personal.

A major reason for this is that one's relationship with Christ is a relationship with one's *own Christ-Self, one's own Father, (YOU)* not some far-off invisible presence; it is as personal as personal can get, as one learns to love themselves as soul, spirit, and Christ within; in addition, the love and care from Christ include satisfying the littlest of needs, to the greatest of gifts, salvation; it could not be more personal and loving.

Furthermore, the love one *feels* from Christ is so intense and incredibly caring, that to call it impersonal misses the mark; Christ is an overwhelming volcano of white hot love; the smallest spark of its fiery lava leaves one weeping uncontrollably; Christ must protect one from too much of this intense flame at once, or the believer would be spiritually incinerated.

There is a caveat to one's perception of this love: this wonderful, indescribable love always does what is right for the believer, not what the believer may want; this may *appear* impersonal; in point of fact, these occurrences are even more personal and caring.

"For whom the LORD loveth he correcteth; even as a father the son *in whom* he delighteth." (Proverbs 3:12)

It is known that when Jesus prayed to His Father, He used the personal pronoun for father; the equivalent in English is daddy.

"He that loveth not knoweth not God; for God is love." (I John 4:8)

The deeper teachings believe that in the kingdom of God, love is the only law there is. In the great commandment, Christ Jesus declares that love supersedes all other laws, and that all other laws come out of this one.

"Nay, in all these things we are more than conquers through him that loved us. For I am persuaded, that neither death, nor life, nor angels, nor principalities, nor powers, nor things present, nor things to come, Nor height, nor depth, nor any other creature, shall be able to separate us from the love of God, which is in Christ Jesus our Lord." (Romans 8:37-39)

Creative imagination

The deeper teachings of Christ believe that one is creating their life: not virtually, but literally. This "creation" depends on one's thoughts, feelings, actions, and most importantly, the imagination. Man is the creator of everything in his life whether he knows it or not; he is the little god of his life.

"Jesus answered them, Is it not written in your law, I said, Ye are Gods?" (John 10:34)

"For as he thinketh in his heart, so *is* he." (Proverbs 23:7)

The means of correct creation in one's life is called "thinking from the end." In other words, one's future goals should be thought of as something already accomplished. If dwelling in the fifth heaven is one's goal, they should imagine themselves as *already* there.

One ignores the present reality of not being there now, and assumes they *are there now;* they then live *as if* they *are* there now. A Christian should also imagine themselves as totally honest, sincere, saved, and anything else they wish to be, *right now,* as already accomplished goals. Such assumptions grow into spiritual fact; this takes spiritual intrepidness.

This entails completely ignoring any present conditions that oppose their wish. It also calls on one to act in accordance with their goal and desire. For example, if one wanted to be totally honest in all things, they must believe that they are totally honest *now,* and *act* accordingly. Let the liar say, I am truthful. In addition, one *must* believe this to be true.

"Jesus answered and said unto them, Verily I say unto you, If ye have faith, and doubt not, ye shall not only do this *which is done* to the fig tree, but also if ye shall say unto this mountain, Be thou removed, and be thou cast into the sea; it shall be done." (Matthew 21:21)

"Jesus said unto him, If thou canst believe, all thing *are* possible to him that believeth." (Mark 9:23)

"Therefore I say unto you, What things soever ye desire, when ye pray, believe that ye receive *them,* and ye shall have *them."* (Mark 11:24)

One is already using their imagination to fashion their own reality, whether they are aware of this principle or not. Every single thing about one has been created this way. Everything they imagine about themselves to be true, has manifested and *become* true. Certainly, one does not want to worry, harbor negativity, or engage in behavior that *creates* an undesirable reality.

Since one cannot help but be creating their reality already, no matter what, one might as well imagine wonderful things about themselves *as* their *present* reality, and then *live* accordingly.

"For as he thinketh in his heart, so *is* he: …." (Proverbs 23:7)

Self-surrender

Surrendering to Christ begins when one accepts Christ as their Father, personal savior, friend, counselor, benefactor, guide, teacher, companion, and eventually, one's very self. Stating what one does is easy; one gives their life up to Christ. This entails giving up one's personal will and ego, and attempting to live a Christ-like life according to His guidance. This brings various spiritual challenges to the surface.

Perhaps the greatest of these challenges is the mind; in the beginning, it does *not* want to cooperate. It does not want to give up its control of one's life. The mind has programmed desires: money; power; fame; love; sex; acceptance; security; respect; family; mate; and *everything* else that tickles its fancy.

The mind and its desires are automatic; technically, the mind and unconscious cannot think; they have been programmed exactly like a computer. The believer must reprogram, retrain, and transform the mind.

The hard news for the believer in the beginning, is that Christ does not want one to focus on worldly desires. It is not that the worldly things are evil in themselves; they are clean if handled correctly, (Romans 14:14) and are there to enjoy.

It is that one's focus should now be on Christ. If one follows through with their spiritual commitment, worldly things will assume the correct perspective in time. However, there will be flash points when one will have to make hard choices; this will take strong self-discipline, *allowing* Christ to do His will through one.

Ideally, one gradually replaces old desires with new spiritual goals, instead of using harsh negation to disconnect from their previous life before Christ. This becomes easier as one begins having experiences with their higher self and Christ, since there is nothing in the world, that can compare to happenings with Christ, which make the brightest gems the world has to offer look as nothing.

"Yea doubtless, and I count all things *but* loss for the excellency of the knowledge of Christ Jesus my Lord: for whom I have suffered the loss of all things, and do count them *but* dung, that I may win Christ, ..." (Philippians 3:8)

Part of this challenge with the mind, involves the fact that the ego will convince the person that they *have* self-surrendered, and that they do not care about worldly desires; subsequently, they continue to pursue their worldly wants believing that they are living a Christ-like life. This problem is extremely difficult to solve. St Paul reminds Christians that the mind *cannot* surrender to the law of God: *cannot!*

"Because the carnal mind *is* enmity against God: for it is not subject to the law of God, neither indeed can be." (Romans 8:7)

The mind is capable of interfering with one's devotions; it will make one so busy, that there is not enough time; interruptions will occur, just as one was about to begin.

To compound the situation, most individuals believe that they are their mind, and that their mind is their soul. The mind revels in this illusion; it loves to pretend that it *is* the soul. This adds to the illusion that they are living Christ-like lives, and that their worldly pursuits are legitimate. They have little idea of how tied to the world they are.

Most of mankind want security with God, *and* their worldly desires. This is quite natural, but Jesus the Christ cautions that this is not possible. Those sincere Christians violating this principle risk being stripped of everything they hold dear, as they are "crucified with Christ"; those insincere Christians violating this principle risk their salvation.

"No man can serve two masters: for either he will hate the one, and love the other; or else he will hold to the one, and despise the other. Ye cannot serve God and mammon." (Matthew 6:24)

As one centers their attention more on Christ, their attachment to the world will naturally fade. Changes made will be made because one wants to make them, and Christ, and one's daily devotions, will make the changes a reality.

Generally, those believers that are attracted to the deeper teachings, have seen through the world, and its hollow promises of happiness. They also want something deeper than mainstream religion is offering. Those individuals dropping out of religion today are not leaving because they no longer believe in Christ: they want something more profound.

A second challenge to self-surrender has already been noted: the mind wants to believe that it is the soul. This is even a more subtle and difficult problem than ridding oneself of worldly desires. This is similar to believing that one's car *is* the driver, and they (as soul) are riding along in the back seat.

Even after viewing its luminous self in the fourth heaven, most Mental Plane residents continue to identify with the mind, instead of identifying as soul. This allows the mind to continue its depravity, slyly pursuing its worldly agenda, while it convinces the individual that they are pure. Souls in the fourth heaven *have* achieved a high degree of purity and truth: however, it is not good enough to enter the kingdom of heaven, nor are they close to the Christ consciousness.

In the fourth heaven, this chimera, mind ruling soul, usually manifests as a desire for recognition and fame; the mind wants to be noticed and listened to; the mind says to itself, "Don't people know who I am? If they would only listen to *me: ME!*" Such individuals love fancy robes, titles, followers, and positions of authority.

"For we wrestle not against flesh and blood, but against principalities, against powers, against rulers of the darkness of this world, against spiritual wickedness in high places." (Ephesians 6:12)

This challenge of identification with the mind is almost insoluble, and it usually takes a prolonged dark night of soul to solve it, along with continuing revelations from Christ and the Holy Spirit, *if* one is willing to listen to them.

Be that as it may, souls in the fourth heaven are extremely happy, and they revel in their mental identification, imagining themselves to be finished with their journey, and residing in the positive God heavens; they will not listen to anything contrary to their belief.

Eventually, Christ will give these souls experiences that will gently move them towards the realization that they are *fully ignorant, totally powerless; irrevocably dependent; unquestionably foolish; absolutely filthy; unbelievably insignificant;* and *grossly unworthy!*

"For all that *is* in the world, the lust of the flesh, and the lust of the eyes, and the pride of life, is not of the Father, but is of the world." (I John 2:16)

This spiritual gauntlet, identification with the mind, is the last major hurdle before being born of the spirit, and entering the Kingdom of God in the fifth heaven; there are uncountable zillions of souls stalled in the fourth heaven that are unable, or unwilling to navigate this dilemma.

As is always the case, one moves forward through realizations and the necessary applications of them. What realizations? That one *is soul*, that deeper essence within that is as pure as the Light of Christ, and *fully* selfless; this is one's true identity.

Those souls that *do* see through the mind and its desires, are in the perfect position to spiritualize their mind, and turn it into a wonderful helpmeet for Christ in their Christian life.

Full self-surrender begins once one receives the Christ consciousness in the fifth heaven: before attaining this magical viewpoint, the believer's perceptive faculties were not acute enough to see numerous flaws and illusions in their own personality; an entirely new level of surrender becomes painfully apparent. This will not be done in a day and a night. One must perceive and correct deep flaws within themselves: very deep flaws.

"And be not conformed to this world: but be ye transformed by the renewing of your mind, that ye may prove what *is* that good, and acceptable, and perfect, will of God." (Romans 12:2)

"Let this mind be in you, which was also in Christ Jesus: …." (Philippians 2:5)

Let go, and let God. The believer *must let* Christ make these changes in one's life.

"In all thy ways acknowledge him, and he shall direct thy paths." (Proverbs 3:6)

Freedom

"And the chief captain answered, With a great sum obtained I this freedom. And Paul said, But I was *free* born." (Acts 22:28)

Freedom *is* happiness, and the differing components of man all want to be free: soul wants to be free; mind wants to be free; emotions want to be free; and, the dark side of man wants to be free. They all want the freedom to do what they want, where they want, and when they want…without interference; there is massive competition between these elements within one.

The challenge of deciding which part of oneself wins out is self-evident. Of course, the Christian wants Christ to be in control. Naturally, one's human consciousness at times is going to protest; battles are going to occur.

Believers following God's will are letting Christ and soul run free; those attached to worldly pleasures are letting their mental and emotional desires run free; those resorting to violence and criminal acts are letting their dark side run free.

Ironically, lost souls are exactly where they are supposed to be, and they are doing the things they cannot help doing; one cannot expect first graders to understand higher grades, and first heaven experiences are what graduate soul into the second heaven.

The tree of the knowledge of good and evil has many branches to climb; there is no way around this; they *must* all be experienced; a skipped branch is a potential trap. How many times soul chooses to experience a branch before learning, is where free will is determinate.

When the Christian is ready to let Christ rule, the most wonderful freedoms become a reality: freedom from worldly desires; freedom from worry; freedom from fear; freedom from death; and freedom from one's own ego, mind, and emotions. This is true freedom, to let Christ's will be one's own will. Those souls inhabiting the kingdom of heaven are free to do whatever they want; the only law is love.

"Thy kingdom come. Thy will be done in earth, as *it is* in heaven." (Matthew 6:10)

"Not everyone that saith unto me, Lord, Lord, shall enter into the kingdom of heaven; but he that doeth the will of my Father, which is in heaven." (Matthew 7:21)

The shadow, or dark side

Every non-Christian, and every Christian, has a dark side, that part of the unconscious that harbors the terrible thoughts and feelings that are too evil to share, even with one's own conscious mind. This is called the shadow or dark side by psychiatrists; it is very powerful, and impossible to fully suppress. It appears in most of one's dreams. The shadow does not care about others, is totally self-absorbed, and means to survive. It has no compunction about cursing, prejudice, violence, sexual perversion, or killing. It is ancient.

It loves rich food, sex, power, anger, violence, vengeance, complaining, and belittling others. Ironically, it is very intelligent, and knows the ugly truth about oneself and others, that is usually so bad it is unspoken. It feels hurt, angry, ignored, and is ready to fight or flee to defend itself. In the Holy Bible, it is associated with the heart.

"The heart is deceitful above all *things,* and desperately wicked: who can know it?" (Jeramiah 17:9)

"But those things which proceed out of the mouth come forth from the heart; and they defile the man. For out of the heart proceed evil thoughts, murders, adulteries, fornications, thefts, false witness, blasphemies: ...." (Matthew 15:18-19)

"For I know that in me (that is, in my flesh,) dwelleth no good thing: for to will is present with me; but how to perform that which is good I find not. For the good that I would I do not: but the evil which I would not, that I do. I find then a law, that, when I would do good, evil is present with me." (Romans 18:19,21)

Many Christians are unaware of this component or pretend it is under control; the naïve do not believe they have a dark side. They will blame the devil for any negative thoughts or actions, and feel guilty for not being able to get rid of its influence.

If one attempts to suppress their shadow, its power increases to the point it will explode, often at the worst time imaginable. Many wonderful Christians have gone down attempting to fully exorcise their dark side. It cannot be done; this component will *not* be ignored.

One may say or do horrible things to their closest relations, and later, regretfully wonder what on Earth got into them. People generally are dumbfounded about acquaintances that snap, claiming they were the most mild-mannered of people.

Strange as it may seem, one needs a relationship with this part of oneself *in order to control it*. Without acknowledging this side of one, the risk of totally losing it is very possible, something one hears about in the news every day.

There are several ways to take the pressure off one's shadow: one might occasionally treat themselves to days off work, rich food, sugar treats, lazy relaxing, love with their mate, or intense physical exercise.

In addition, when wronged, it is important to speak up and express what is bothering one; swallowing anger merely postpones the release of it, and continuing to suppress it risks a larger and more vicious explosion down the road.

It is better to simply tell the truth about a problem in a calm, objective way, rather than waiting until one is so mad, that they will blurt out exaggerated grievances and wild charges, or commit a terrible act. Telling the truth that the dark side knows, and wants to get out, will relieve its pressure. The shadow is supra-sensitive and deeply defensive; it looks to take offense.

Prayer and devotions will also help understand this challenge, and the believer will receive help from the Lord in controlling it. This part of one does not change or evolve; however, if acknowledged and understood, it can be integrated into one's spiritual life.

It should not be that hard to understand this part of oneself: after all, everyone has been under the control of it so very many times.

"Let all bitterness, and wrath, and anger, and clamour, and evil speaking, be put away from you, with all malice: …." (Ephesians 4:31)

It is also helpful to be careful about who one unloads their anger on, lest they invite a response they regret. Perhaps one might focus their anger on an alternative target, such as beating a plastic dummy, or destroying a cardboard box. Jesus, when angered by commerce in the temple, overturned tables and chairs, scattered their money on the floor, and chased the guilty out of the temple with a whip of cords (scourge) He had made. (Matthew 21:12)

If one is aware of this side of oneself, and has established somewhat of a relationship with it, giving it some space and understanding, ironically, there are huge benefits: one is more *confident* in the Lord;

one is more *truthful* in their dealings with others; they are *braver* in those spiritual or physical interactions requiring intrepidness; they are more *forgiving* of foibles in themselves and others; they are better able to *control* themselves in heated situations; their *understanding* of themselves, and life, is measurably increased; they are more *complete* and *integrated*. They are closer to Christ.

Worship of the personality

"And whosoever shall exalt himself shall be abased; and he that shall humble himself shall be exalted." (Matthew 23:12)

In the world today, most people worship and idolize man. It may be political figures, movie stars, sports stars, musicians, beautiful women, or famous personalities; this is often called the worship of the personality. There is no mention of God or Christ in this worship, as though the individuals lionized have done it all themselves, instead of giving the credit to God, who has *done it all* through them.

"He that speaketh of himself seeketh his own glory: but he that seeketh his glory that sent him, the same is true, and no unrighteousness is in him." (John 7:18)

Those who receive this deification strut about as though they deserve such recognition, or smile with false modesty as though it were nothing; this is ignorance and spiritual death. The secret teachings refer to this as the worship of Moloch, the Old Testament heathen deity, that the Israelites worshiped when astray from God. They gloried in the works of their own creation, while sacrificing human beings.

"And they made a calf in those days, and offered sacrifice unto the idol, and rejoiced in the works of their own hands." (Acts 7:41)

"And he said unto them, Ye are they which justify yourselves before men; but God knoweth your hearts: for that which is highly esteemed among men is abomination in the sight of God." (Luke 16:15)

"And upon a set day Herod, arrayed in royal apparel, sat upon his throne, and made an oration unto them. And the people gave a shout, *saying, It is* the voice of a god, and not of a man. And immediately the angel of the Lord smote him, because he gave not God the glory: and he was eaten of worms, and gave up the ghost." (Acts 12:21-23)

If one wishes to know how acknowledgement should be handled, one only has to study the words of Jesus the Christ. He continuously refuses to take a shred of credit for *anything,* and gives God the credit in dozens of different ways; it is a point He will not let go of; He will *not* even let himself be called a "good man."

"And he said unto him, Why callest me good? *there is* none good but one, *that is, God*: ...." (Matthew 19:17)

"Believest thou not that I am in the Father, and the Father in me? The words that I speak unto you I speak not of myself: but the Father that dwelleth in me, he doeth the works." (John 14:10)

"I can of my own self do nothing: as I hear, I judge: and my judgement is just; because I seek not my own will, but the will of the Father which sent me." (John 5:30)

"Then said Jesus unto them, When ye have lifted up the Son of man, then shall ye know that I am *he,* and *that* I do nothing of myself; but as my Father has taught me." (John 8:28)

There is a hierarchy of how things successively manifest in Creation: *all* things emanate from God, and subsequently manifest as Christ, which then proceeds as Spirit; next, they manifest as Soul; subsequently, soul projects itself through the unconscious body, the high mental body, the causal body, the lower mental body, the astral body, the lunar body, and finally, manifests in the human body and physical consciousness, which desires to take the entire credit for *everything* and *anything* that occurs.

"And when he had called the people *unto him* with his disciples also, he said unto them, Whosoever will come after me, let him deny himself, and take up his cross, and follow me." (Mark 8:34)

"And whosoever shall exalt himself shall be abased; and he that shall humble himself shall be exalted." (Matthew 23:12)

After one has been crucified with Christ, one humbly assumes the proper perspective; one is a grain of dust "scattered before the wind." The wonder of it is that said grain of dust can be fulfilled, no matter its level of growth, and live in unspeakable joy in Christ.

The feminine believer

"There is neither Jew nor Greek, there is neither bond nor free, there is neither male nor female: for ye are all one in Christ Jesus." (Galatians 3:28)

The deeper secret wisdom does not differentiate between men and women: they are treated equally in *all* respects. In addition, beginning with the fifth heaven, there are no men and women; the two souls have become one and they "…neither marry, nor are given in marriage: Neither can they die any more: for they are equal unto the angels; and are the children of God, being the children of the resurrection." (Luke: 20:35-36)

Furthermore, the hidden teachings do not have churches or temples: it is an individual, solitary journey. This means that there are not worldly, spiritual authorities over one asking for obedience, which is an affront to soul. This freedom also extends to marriage; the deeper teachings do not recognize one sex ruling over the other in any capacity whatsoever; such would also be an affront to soul.

Many women today are in restrictive, subservient positions with little freedom. This is not Christ's way. The deeper teachings can provide solace, as there is freedom on the *inside* with Christ, that if desired, no one need know. Women face the same choice as men: go with the world or go with Christ.

Detachment

Detachment means not caring unnecessarily about the world, family, persons, mate …. This is mainly an emotional detachment from the worldly life. This does not mean becoming cold, or shirking any responsibilities; it means that the things of the world have lost much of their relative importance, and count as little next to one's life with Christ: in other words, having the correct perspective. This is an aspect of living in peace.

Who cares who is president or what crazy things the public is doing. These worldly events do not have to affect one. Of course, it is important to love those close to one, but one can broaden their perspective on that as well: Who were one's family last lifetime, or the uncountable lifetimes before that? It is possible one's "extended" family contains everyone on Earth in this "generation": they are *all* one's children, parents, and siblings. One's present children are no more special than anyone else's children.

The sincere Christian can rest in the knowledge that Christ is in charge of *everything* in their life, and lets nothing happen that is not part of His plan. This promise will test one to their limits, and many are quick to utter "why me God?" when things go south. It demands trust; however, this knowledge, that Christ is in charge, is relaxing and peace giving.

"And we know that all things work together for good to them that love God, to them who are the called according to *his* purpose." (Romans 8:28)

One receives insight in to Christ Jesus' attitude towards others when he is asked a question:

"And they sent out unto him their disciples with the Herodians, saying, Master, we know that thou art true, and teachest the way of God in truth, neither carest thou for any *man:* for thou regardest not the person of men." (Matthew 22:16)

Sometimes, spiritual love can look rather cold but it is not; however, it is less emotional than personal love, and perhaps the opposite of romance. It is a fusion of personal and impersonal aspects; It is good will towards all with an openness that is ready to help. It is fair, objective, and does not play favorites. It can become personal in a second.

This does not rule out personal love for family and those close to one; it increases and focuses it. One *cannot* give personal love to everyone; one *can* give impersonal love to everyone.

Becoming detached about the world is the equivalent of withdrawing from the world. This saves tremendous emotional energy, which can be applied to power those spiritual things one *does* care about.

"Perverse disputings of men of corrupt minds, and destitute of the truth, supposing that gain is godliness: from such withdraw thyself." (I Timothy 6:5)

Dreams and visions

The secret teachings believe that dreams and visions are one of the primary ways that Christ, and soul, teach the physical consciousness spiritual lessons. Dreams are made up of symbols and metaphors, whereas visions may be reality, but seen through one's inner eyes.

"For God speaketh once, yea twice, *yet man* perceiveth it not. In a dream, in a vision of the night, when deep sleep falleth upon men, in slumberings upon the bed; Then he openeth the ears of men, and sealeth their instruction. That he may withdraw man *from his* purpose, and hide pride from man." (Job 33:14-17)

The Holy Bible contains many famous dreams using symbols and metaphors, such as Pharaoh's dream of seven fat cattle, eaten by seven lean ones, which presaged the coming of a great seven-year famine. (Genesis 41:1-4)

There are also many famous visions in the Holy Word, such as Saul's vision of Jesus the Christ on the road to Damascus; such visions are considered reality. (Acts 9:3-7)

"And he said, Hear now my words: If there be a prophet among you, *I* the LORD will make myself known unto him in a vision, *and* will speak unto him in a dream." (Numbers 12:6)

Once an individual sincerely accepts Christ as their savior, their dream world will change. Whereas before Christ, dreams were usually a struggle between the various components of man, working to integrate themselves into a united harmonic whole, after accepting Christ, the individual's dream life will primarily be lessons and guidance from the Holy Spirit, and one's own higher self. Christ will insure that the sincere believer's dream-life is true.

These dreams will have to be interpreted and applied. This is simpler than expected, since during spiritual contemplation of the dream, Christ will give you the answers. As stated, soul communicates in dreams to the human consciousness using metaphors; once this is realized, interpretation is easier.

For example: a girl had argued with her mother over staying out later in the evening. That night, the young girl dreamed one image: her mother was putting a coat around her (daughter's) shoulders. In reflecting on the dream, the daughter realized that her mother was simply trying to protect her.

Some dreams bring back the exact feeling one had in a past catastrophe; perhaps one is being asked to address that situation, and hopefully bleed and resolve it.

If one is new to dream interpretation, a good dream book or app is helpful to get started. The deeper teaching's views are similar to Jungian interpretations, which are very akin to spiritual science; esoteric beliefs do not favor Freudian interpretations.

Spiritual dreams are usually simple to interpret and very clear; Christ wants one to "get it." If a dream is really difficult to interpret, it usually is not worth it, and if an important dream-message is missed, soul will send it again in another way. Lessons and messages from within occur along the lines of one's own personality; everyone is different.

There are parts of one's overall constitution that are dreaming all night, but these are usually dreams that disappear from memory immediately upon waking. A spiritual dream will be clear and often unforgettable. If it is a problem-solving dream, and ninety percent of spiritual dreams are, the issue will be presented with an accompanying solution, usually in the last segment of the dream.

One must be careful not to see what they desire in dreams, and interpret them objectively. This can be challenging, as the dream can *seem* real, especially upon awaking, and the dreamer may want to interpret the dream literally.

For instance, the people in one's dreams are seldom people in one's life; instead, they stand for qualities in one's own personality that soul is drawing one's attention to. That person in one's dream who is disliked because of their coldness, is referring to one's own lack of warmth, *not* the individual pictured in the dream.

Dream events may also be symbolic: a dream of pregnancy may presage a spiritual birth; a dream of death may foretell the demise of an old habit; a dream image of a white dove may symbolize the Holy Spirit.

Once one understands soul's use of puns, symbols, metaphors, associations, jokes, and other unique ways of delivering a message via dreams, and the dreamer asks: "Father, what are you telling me here?" the answers will come during peaceful contemplation.

Visions are usually more memorable than dreams, and often contain a heightened sense of reality; they seem more real and they often *are*. Visions may or may not include figurative devices. At times, it may seem that there is little difference between a vision and dream. The most important visions usually involve viewings of one's luminous selves, or visions of the Christ.

There is no method or technique to force a spiritual dream or vision; they are given by Christ through soul, and will come through the Lord's grace at the proper time when one is ready. Of course, it never hurts to ask.

It can be humorous for soul to communicate with the human consciousness; it is similar to a human being attempting to message an ant. None the less, dreams from soul are so clever and creative, that the recipient is usually amazed, and has little trouble in interpreting the message. There is no limit to spirit's profundity and creativity; everything goes: puns, symbols, associations, names, cosmic events, brilliant metaphors and similes, powerful feelings and emotions, buried memories, and more.

Recording one's dream is considered profitable, as some dreams appear in a series over time, and one dream may help interpret earlier dreams. It also allows one to see their own growth in consciousness, as they expand their awareness in Christ. Sometimes, one receives new insights from contemplating an old dream; being removed from when the dream occurred, puts one in a better position to interpret it objectively.

Spiritual dreams do not occur very often, and they occur less and less as soul ascends to inner regions that are out of dream's scope. In addition, as the believer grows in Christ, they are able to better hear His voice, and soul does not have to fashion a dream message.

Life on Earth is a dream, and one can interpret events in one's life, as though they are a dream. Soul needs to awake and realize it is not the "earthy man," but the "Lord from heaven."

Visions are rarer and are wonderful gifts from Christ. He gives one as much time as needed to understand what the believer has experienced; they are life-changing.

"And it shall come to pass in the last days, saith God, I will pour out of my Spirit upon all flesh: and your sons and your daughters shall prophecy, and your young men shall see visions, and your old men shall dream dreams." (Acts 2:17)

Faith

"And Jesus answering saith unto them, Have faith in God." (Mark 11:22)

"But without faith *it is impossible* to please *him:* for he that cometh to God must believe that he is, and *that* he is a rewarder of them that diligently seek him." (Hebrews 11:6)

Faith in Christ is one of the essentials for believers, and without it, there will be little if any growth, especially in the beginning of one's Christian journey. Christ in Jesus is constantly calling out the disciples and others over their lack of faith.

"And immediately Jesus stretched forth *his* hand, and caught him, and said unto him, O thou of little faith, wherefore didst thou doubt?" (Matthew 14:31)

"*Which* when Jesus perceived, he said unto them, O ye of little faith, why reason ye among yourselves, because ye have brought no bread?" (Matthew 16:8)

"And he said unto them, Why are ye so fearful? How is it that ye have no faith?" (Mark 4:40)

On the affirmative side, Christ Jesus repeatedly states that many He healed, *were* healed because of their faith.

"But Jesus turned him about, and when he saw her, he said, Daughter, be of good comfort; thy faith hath made thee whole. And the woman was made whole from that hour." (Matthew 9:22)

"When Jesus saw their faith, he said unto the sick of the palsy, Son, thy sins be forgiven thee." (Mark 2:5)

"And Jesus said unto him, Go thy way; thy faith hath made thee whole. And immediately he received his sight and followed Jesus in the way." (Mark 10:52)

Christ Jesus also suggests that there are degrees of faith; it is not necessarily an all or nothing virtue.

"Then touched he their eyes, saying, According to your faith be it unto you." (Matthew 9:29)

When the disciples ask Jesus, why they could not cast out a devil from an afflicted man, Jesus tells them they did not believe they could do it.

"And Jesus said unto them, Because of your unbelief: for verily I say unto you, If ye have faith as a grain of mustard seed, ye shall say unto this mountain, Remove hence to yonder place; and it shall remove; and nothing shall be impossible to you." (Matthew 17:20)

"He that is faithful in that which is least is faithful also in much: and he that is unjust in the least is unjust also in much." (Luke 16:10)

Perhaps one of the most accepted, and most repeated definitions of faith, is found in Hebrews:

"Now faith is the substance of things hoped for, the evidence of things not seen." (Hebrews 11:1)

Faith is needed by the believer for so many things. For example, one must have faith that God will provide, and that He will lead one in His ways. However, the deeper teachings of Christ also believe that for those fanatics deep in Christ, they *will see,* not only their own higher selves, but Christ Himself in all His glory.

Consequently, their faith will have been rewarded, and aspects of their journey will no longer *need* faith, as they will be granted sight of things above in visions and dreams. They will *know.* This is happening all over the globe for uncountable believers.

"He that hath my commandments, and keepeth them, he it is that loveth me: and he that loveth me shall be loved of my Father, and I will love him, and will manifest myself to him." (John 14:21)

"And he said, Hear now my words: If there be a prophet among you, I the Lord will make myself known unto him in a vision, *and* will speak unto him in a dream." (Numbers 12:6)

Faith can be difficult to acquire on one's own, especially when spiritual things have remained unseen. The deeper doctrine believes that it comes from Christ, and that there is nothing untoward about directly asking Christ for more faith.

"And the apostles said unto the Lord, Increase our faith." (Luke 17:5)

"And straightway the father of the child cried out, and said with tears, Lord I believe; help thou mine unbelief." (Mark 9:2)

There is a central realization that greatly aids the believer's faith in Christ: Creation is absolutely, without exception, stunningly perfect. God is perfect; Christ is perfect; the Word is perfect; every level of heaven is perfect; and, every soul is exactly at the place it must be. Granted, this is counterintuitive, but divinely true none the less. Of course, this must be explained.

For example, war is thought to be an ultimate evil, yet as explained earlier, Christ Jesus states that He has brought the sword and war on purpose. It is part of Christ's lessons on what good and evil are, and experience is the teacher. Souls learn that war is evil by going to war. What soul learns is important, bodies are expendable.

"Think not that I am come to send peace on earth: I came not to send peace, but a sword." (Matthew 10:34)

"Suppose ye that I am come to give peace on earth? I tell you nay; but rather division: For from henceforth there shall be five in one house divided, three against two, and two against three. The father shall be divided against the son, and the son against the father; the mother against the daughter, and the daughter against the mother; the mother in law against her daughter in law; and the daughter in law against her mother in law." (Luke 12:51-53)

A secondary realization, that accompanies seeing into the Lord's masterplan, is that human bodies are of little concern. It is the soul, the deeper consciousness within one, that is of primary importance; it is the true experiencer of life. Bodies that souls inhabit come and go like the wind as lifetimes sail by, changing like people change their clothes. One hundred million souls lost their body in world war II; not one soul perished.

"Now I say, brethren, that flesh and blood cannot inherit the kingdom of God; neither doth corruption inherit incorruption." (I Corinthians 15:50)

In addition, on a more personal level, the terrible things like rape, accidents and murder are also spiritually explainable. Souls that are beginners in a human body, and have no moral compass, initiate violent actions and experiences, that wake up and vivify their inner bodies; these consciousness centers, in the beginning, are only dormant potentialities; they can only can respond to gross outer vibrations and events.

The severe consequences for such actions, which they chose through free will, teach souls hard lessons, further waking up consciousness centers in their inner bodies. Their bad choices are pitted against other souls making bad choices, and no one has anything happen to themselves that they have not earned and created; this is absolute. Evil comes from man, and returns to man.

Bad things happen to those who have created bad things; good things happen to those who have created good. However, on Earth, no person is that good, which means most everyone reaps numerous hard, spiritual lessons. Jesus said that no one is good, including Himself.

"And he [Jesus] said unto him, Why callest me good? *there is* none good but one, *that is,* God: ...." (Matthew 19:17)

Furthermore, the Lord's justice system is exact, and carried forward from life to life, until one graduates from the lower heavens. "So called" good and bad come back to one exactly as they are created; understanding this principle is one of the keys to the good life: life with Christ, in Christ, and as Christ's servant.

"But seek ye first the kingdom of God, and his righteousness; and all these things shall be added unto you." (Matthew 6:33)

"Be not deceived; God is not mocked: for whatsoever a man soweth, that shall he also reap." (Galatians 6:7)

The overall point is this: there is *no evil* other than what man creates for himself, and when one sees the perfection of Christ's creation, one can have *faith* that all is in place for themselves as well; there is no chaos; *everything* in one's life, including accepting Christ, is part of their own individual plan and destiny.

"And he said, Therefore said I unto you, that no man can come unto me, except it were given unto him of my Father." (John 6:65)

For sincere Christians, this verse is a wonderful confirmation; they have been called by God.

A miracle of miracles, is that all of the individual souls in creation, with their own individual place, plan, and destiny, interrelate without interference, and the creation hums along perfectly. Christ *is* perfect; one can have faith that everything is precisely in place.

"This then is the message which we have heard of him, and declare unto you, that God is light, and in him is no darkness at all." (I John 1:5)

Present Times

From 1938 to 1945, a tremendous planetary sacrifice occurred. Five hundred million souls either had their bodies killed or grievously wounded. Trillions of dollars in destruction occurred and incalculable suffering. This blood sacrifice set the stage and *paid* for a far-reaching spiritual renewal, and a transformation of Earth's consciousness: this dispensation from Christ began a golden period that will last one thousand years.

In a relatively short time, new countries were formed; a relative peace was established; the United Nations was created; the Atomic age began; space exploration was initiated; new technology exploded; weapons were designed that could destroy humanity; transistors were invented; computers were designed; the internet was created; hand-held computer/phones became the norm; a space station orbiting the planet was established; trips to Mars were planned; the planet began heating and spinning faster; glaciers began melting; Earth's health became a concern; the rights of women and minorities garnered reforms; animals became people too; the secret teachings became widely available.

Thousands of highly evolved souls in Christ began incarnating on the planet, working to establish the foundation of a new spiritual consciousness; additionally, many souls incarnated to further their own personal spiritual advancement, hoping to take advantage of this spiritual attention by Christ.

This Christly renaissance has affected *every* field of endeavor; in addition. thousands of new groups seeking closeness with God have sprung up planet-wide, like lovely lilies in the light. This renewal will also include meeting those from other planets, whose *public* arrival is imminent.

The incarnation of highly evolved souls has greatly impacted the world consciousness, primarily due to their communion with God. It has also refreshed and strengthened high states of spiritual consciousness, that are filled with Christ's love and wisdom. This makes it easier for other souls to attract these realizations and spiritual states of consciousness, making Christ and profound truths more available to every soul on Earth.

This will increasingly lead to the continued fading of religion, as millions of believers are switching from following "outer" spiritual rituals and authorities, to going *within* themselves for a more personal relationship with Christ, and the kingdom of heaven.

"God that made the world and all things therein, seeing that he is Lord of heaven and Earth, dwelleth not in temples made with hands; …." (Acts 17:24)

"And when he was demanded of the Pharisees, when the kingdom of God should come, he answered them and said, The kingdom of God cometh not with observation: Neither shall they say Lo here, or, Lo there! for, behold, the kingdom of God is within you." (Luke 17:20-21)

Those looking for worldly peace and harmony during a spiritual millennium, are looking for the wrong things: the world will always be in travail. The availability of spiritual teachings, and increased awareness, are what make a "millennium" golden. The many worldly improvements, *and* disasters, are simply the secondary effects of this increase in consciousness.

Worldly persons do not perceive this spiritual millennium; they believe things are worse than ever, and if focusing on worldly events they may be right, as the negative energies needed, to balance this positive spiritual renaissance are colossal: earthquakes, volcanic eruptions, tsunamis, cyclones, tornados, famine, war, dictators, plagues, drugs, crime and horrifying tragedies; the planet Earth, like everything else in the lower dual heavens, is kept in perfect balance between the positive and negative forces. When the positive increases ….

CONCLUSION

This brief overview of the deeper secret teachings of Christ, contains some of the deepest spiritual truths known to man, and if followed, will eventually result not only in full salvation, but in the believer someday *realizing* their Christ-Self, at the very top of Jacob's ladder.

Every rung of Jacob's ladder brings happiness and fulfilment if lived in Christ, and it is not necessary to be at the top to be in spiritual bliss. Souls in human bodies are already so very close to Christ, whether they realize it or not. *Every* soul is satisfied to be as it is, and if lived correctly, can be fulfilled.

All souls will eventually reach the seventh heaven, as this is the ALMIGHTY'S wish (Matthew 18:14); however, that could be some time away. For those intrepid souls that wish to advance more quickly, and leave this relative hell, the sacred highway is open, as the Divine Power is looking for those that wish to become one with It.

"But the hour cometh, and now is, when the true worshippers shall worship the Father in spirit and in truth: for the Father seeketh such to worship him." (John 4:23)

It is easy to describe how to grow in Christ, and following it can be easy as well, if one lets Christ live through them. Learn to *recognize Christ's* voice, and *follow* it through sincere trial and error, with all of one's might.

"Hear, O Israel: The Lord our God *is* one Lord: And thou shalt love the Lord thy God with all thine heart, and with all thy soul, and with all thy might." (Deuteronomy 6:4-5)

"Thou shall not avenge, nor bear any grudge against the children of thy people, but thou shall love thy neighbor as thyself: I am the Lord." (Leviticus 19:18)

"Jesus said unto him, Thou shalt love the Lord thy God with all thy heart, and with all thy soul, and with all thy mind. This is the first and great commandment. And the second *is* like unto it, Thou shalt love thy neighbor as thyself." (Matthew 22:37-39)

GLOSSARY

Atman: The Eastern religions' (Hinduism, Sikhism, Jainism) name for the high soul of man, which dwells in the sixth heaven, never descending below that point. It projects atoms of itself (the low soul) into the lower heavens for experience and realization. The low soul's mission is to realize itself and reunite with its own high soul in the spiritual heavens. The low soul, ignorant and innocent, eats from the tree of the knowledge of good and evil, eventually turns to Christ, and returns to the garden of Eden to eat from the tree of life, rejoining itself as the "Lord of heaven." (I Corinthians 15:47) Atman has no form, and is one with the Holy Spirit.

Audible Sound Current: The Word, the Holy Spirit, the Spirit of God, the Voice of God, the Song of God. The deeper teachings believe that the Holy Spirit can be heard with the inner ears, as these currents go through one's bodies and energy centers (*chakras*). The sounds are very high, very faint, and continuous. One may here one predominant note or multiple sounds. Soul can communicate with the human consciousness using these sounds. Jesus the Christ states that those born of the Holy Spirit can hear the Holy Spirit. (John 3:8)

Augoeides: The viewing of the luminous self. At several points in soul's growth, usually beginning in the fourth heaven, the physical consciousness shares in the experience of viewing its own glorified higher selves. One sees with their own eyes their true identity. (I Corinthians 15:49) Jesus was transfigured in front of three of His disciples, allowing them to see His Luminous Self, "whose face did shine as the sun, and his raiment was white as the light." (Matthew 17:2) These usually happen at milestones in soul's growth.

Awareness: The reception and recognition in the physical consciousness of soul's knowingness, realization, and understanding. One's *level* of awareness is their true spiritual I.Q. Awareness is not intelligence but a deeper level of knowingness and perception that comes from deep within.

Christ: A Spirit that is the entirety of the Word, Creation, and everything manifest; Christ creates all, is all, is in all, sustains all, and is *THEE* Son/Daughter of God. Christ has manifested Itself at infinite levels of Itself, fashioning the seven heavens and *everything* in them, without exception. (John1:3) Christ resides in the Heart of God, unmanifested.

Christ Consciousness: The wonderful consciousness from the fifth heaven and above, referred to as "the mind of Christ." This viewpoint is a deep, intuitive, penetrating level of perception, originating from the innermost part of one's being. One may receive messages and realizations from it in devotions and rare situations; soul is permanently granted the first level of the Christ consciousness upon attaining full salvation in the fifth heaven.

Christ Realization: When the spirit of man reaches the seventh heaven, the prodigal son has returned to his Father, merging with Christ and becoming a Son of God. (John (1:12) The entire spiritual journey to Christ happens *within* one, and *without*, as man explores and masters the same level in his inner and outer universes simultaneously. The kingdom of heaven is *within you*. (Luke 17:20-21)

Consciousness: There are two consciousness's in man, the physical state of being, dependent on the sense organs, and soul's state of being, which is totally independent from the physical mind's activity. A third consciousness is the Christ consciousness. The Holy Spirit is also consciousness, manifesting in infinite states and levels, as there is nothing in creation that is not conscious to some degree.

All consciousness comes from soul and higher, as the mind, being a programed machine, is technically not conscious.

Contemplation: A mixture of focused thinking and pauses in thinking. This combination of thought and the absence of thought, sets the table for guidance and realizations from divine sources within, which occur during pauses in thought. The mind cannot discover the deeper mysteries by thinking; it must receive them by suspending thought, and opening themselves up with the utmost receptivity. "Peace, be still." (Mark 4:39)

Disciple/teacher: A soul that has reached the fifth heaven, and is qualified to help others on their spiritual journey. These disciples have attained the first level of the Christ consciousness and can help students both in their life during the day, and at night when the sleeping student is in their astral body, or higher. These teachers are a paragon of ethical standards. They only help and support, *never* command. They are very rare, perhaps one out of ten thousand spiritual teachers. St. Francis de Assisi is such an example. One desires guidance from Christ before working with any teacher.

Divine Self: The Christ Self, dwelling in the seventh heaven. When soul/spirit reaches this point, and merges with its Christ-Self, it becomes a Son of God. This is the highest point in manifest Creation, and a description of the consciousness at this level is impossible: The divine self is omniscient; omnipotent; omnipresent; ecstatic.

Heart of God: Dark and soundless regions above (within) the seven heavens of manifest creation. It is the home of Watchers, Silent Ones, and Archangels, of which there are uncountable zillions. This is also the dwelling place of the ALMIGHTY ABSOLUTE GOD. The Holy Spirit, not yet manifest, emanates from this region. One meets, blends and merges with their Christ-Self here.

Holy Spirit: The indescribable power and energy that emanates from God, traveling to the very end of creation, and then back to its original departure point, creating and sustaining everything in existence; the ultimate truth and reality. Souls ride the returning waves of the Holy Spirit into the heavens within.

Jesus the Christ: Incarnation from the Heart of God, a Son of God. Jesus was one with His Father, (John 10:30) and *as* Christ, changed the entire planet, opening the way for others to become Sons and Daughters of God. (John 1:12) His teachings, as a direct channel of Christ, are universal, and apply to all levels, kingdoms, and heavens. While containing multiple levels of truth, they are also the essence of truth.

Jiva: The Eastern religions' (Hinduism, Sikhism, Jainism) name for the low soul. This consciousness is creative atoms descended from its own high soul; it usually resides in the causal body, and is generally known as the soul of man. Its presence in the body is responsible for a reflective consciousness in the human body, often *called* the human soul. Eventually, as it progresses, the low soul (jiva) moves into its mental body in the fourth heaven; further growth places it in the soul body in the fifth heaven, and from there it progresses to the sixth heaven, where the low soul (Jiva) and the high soul (Atman) merge and become one, having shed all lower sheaths that protected the low soul in the lower heavens.

Karma: the doctrine that one reaps what one sows; what goes around, comes around. This system includes *both* good and bad, and is held to be exceedingly exact, playing out over lifetimes. It teaches soul that there are consequences to its choices and actions. Karma is not assigned but automatically created by returning creative energies. This is simply Newton's third law of motion applied to *all* energy transfers, physical and psychic. The gospels are exceedingly clear on this principle. (Galatians 6:5-8) Soul escapes this system in the lower heavens by attaining salvation.

Light: The audible Word vibrates, reflecting as Light on the atoms moving in space; light is beauty, intelligence, realization, wisdom, and awareness. All creation in the seven heavens is light and sound.

Meditation: The absence of *all* thought; complete stillness. Although meditation can be very beneficial, the deeper teachings do not favor meditation over contemplation for several reasons. Some who meditate, especially in the East, are *attempting* to *attain* higher states, or some other goal. This is often counter-productive; states, such as the Christ consciousness, *cannot* be won or attained by meditation, or *any* other method whatsoever. They are given by the grace of Christ, after one has *applied* years of guidance, and conformed themselves to Christ. The deeper teachings favor spiritual contemplation, as the best natural way to receive Christ's guidance and instruction. It is not passive, as meditation is; it is a balance of action and no action, focused thought and the absence of thought.

Repentance: A change in direction. One decides to go with Christ instead of their own personal will.

Salvation: Full salvation begins in the fourth heaven upon the viewing of one's radiant self; the low soul sees its own glorified high soul, in its soul body. It has seen with its own eyes who it is. The next steps involve the low soul casting off its mental identification, and merging with the luminous celestial being it witnessed, thus achieving full salvation, and the Christ consciousness, in the fifth heaven, the beginning of the kingdom of God. This is being born of the spirit. In the East, this glorious step is termed self-realization, as one has *realized* their true identity: soul. Subsequently, after further growth, soul realizes that it is spirit. Eventually, spirit realizes that it *is* Christ. These steps are attained through direct experience and realization, and the integration of progressively deeper and more profound consciousness's.

Sin: When a person does something *they* know is wrong. The deeper teachings do not believe one is born in sin; one will have both positive and negative karma. The more evolved souls have much good karma, and very little bad; the less evolved souls …. Soul gets above karma by attaining the fifth heaven.

Soul: Soul is eternal and has the ability to see, hear, perceive, imagine, and have an opinion; it also has a sense of humor. It cannot die or be maimed. It can be lost. The high soul, which stays in the sixth heaven, sends atoms of it consciousness (low soul) into bodies in the lower heavens, for realizations, experiences, and ultimately, the ability to channel Christ throughout the seven heavens. It has no form or movement and cannot be located in time and space. Soul chooses its mission to assist God's cause.

THE SEVEN HEAVENS OF CREATION

PHYSICAL PLANE   1
This is the home of planet Earth, and is technically a sub-plane of the Astral Worlds. Soul at this level is trapped by worldly desires and passions. This plane is dark, nine tenths negative, and one tenth positive. Soul looks out instead of in, and becomes lost in the world, not aware that it is a potential son (daughter) of God. Evil abounds: deep, hard lessons.

ASTRAL PLANE   2
Home of the emotions, desires and passions. Long lifetimes; varied sub planes, from Purgatory at the lower ends of the sub planes, to beautiful templed levels at the top. Identification with family, mate, groups. The emotions range from base desires to deep love for God. The negative pole of creation, much control needed, using emotions for love of Christ.

LOW MENTAL PLANE   3
Basic mind functions, senses etc. Concrete thinking, literal interpretations, many heavens here, souls ready to reincarnate from here after mental integration, move into causal body.

CAUSAL PLANE
Stored memories, karmic patterns, abstract thinking, home of low soul, figurative interpreting.

HIGH MENTAL PLANE	4

Above reincarnation, home of religions, philosophies, morals, ethics, aesthetics. Soul sees Its own radiant self here, the first stage of salvation. Souls here are trapped by the mind and must realize they are soul. Dark night of soul occurs here, intuitive discernment needed. UNCONSCIOUS PLANE (subconscious) No mind area, primitive drives, instinct, intuition.

SOUL PLANE	5

Neutral zone, dividing area between psychic/spiritual worlds, full salvation, self-realization; first level of Christ consciousness: soul has returned to the Garden of Eden, eaten from the tree of life, become immortal, and is one with spirit. Sound of a flute, no space or time.

SPIRIT PLANE	6

Home of high soul, (Atman), soul transitioning to spirit, first positive heaven, endless, clean, diminished form, increased perception, huge missions for Christ, total peace and loveliness.

NAMELESS PLANE	7

Realization of eternity, home of God's power, souls created here, infinite ocean of realized sons of God, they are one with Christ, possess the Christ consciousness, are totally aware, and are ecstatic. The prodigal son has returned home to a glorious welcome from the Father.

HEART OF GOD

Totally dark, totally soundless, home of the Almighty, Archangels, and Silent Watchers. The Word (Christ) emanates from this region. All is present but unmanifested, circumscribes all.

www.ingramcontent.com/pod-product-compliance
Lightning Source LLC
LaVergne TN
LVHW041851070526
838199LV00045BB/1535